THE SUN AT
MIDDAY

THE SUN AT MIDDAY

TALES OF A MEDITERRANEAN FAMILY

GINI ALHADEFF

THE ECCO PRESS

Copyright © 1997 by Gini Alhadeff

THE ECCO PRESS
100 West Broad Street
Hopewell, New Jersey 08525

Published simultaneously in Canada by
Penguin Books Canada, Ltd., Ontario

Reprinted by arrangement with Pantheon Books, a division of Random House,
Inc. A portion of this book was published previously by *Travel & Leisure* magazine.

Printed in the United States of America

Library of Congress Cataloging-in-Publication Data

Alhadeff, Gini.
    The sun at midday : tales of a Mediterranean family / Gini
Alhadeff. — 1st Ecco ed.
        p.   cm.
    ISBN 0-88001-578-0 (paperback)
    1. Alhadeff family. 2. Pinto family. 3. Jews—Italy—Biography.
4. Jews—Egypt—Alexandria—Biography. 5. Sephardim—Biography.
6. Jewish Christians—Biography.   I. Title.
DS135.I9A43   1997b
962'.1—dc21   97-16761
[B]   r97

Book design by Paul Davis

9 8 7 6 5 4 3 2 1

FIRST ECCO EDITION 1998

For Francesco Pellizzi

I shall see an end of faith, nothing
to be beleeved that I doe not know . . .

— John Donne

From A Sermon
Preached at a Marriage,
30 May 1621

THE SUN AT MIDDAY

I

The Sephardi Mediterranean from which I come is a world of many languages and no borders. My father's family speak Ladino among themselves; my mother's speak French. Most of them have a "foreign" accent in every language they speak, though they speak very fluently. Contained in this trace of an accent, in this shred of difference, is the nature of their identity: belonging everywhere, but not quite. In Tuscany, my father is *il signore cinese* and in Italy, though we are Italian by passport, our Arabic surname, often mistaken for Russian, makes us all foreigners. We were never more Italian, in fact, than when we were in Japan because there it meant nothing that our surname did not end in a vowel.

Language to us is not neutral: it is a place, an identity, and a filter. My father uses it to establish fleeting complicities with waiters, cabdrivers, doormen. He can do so in seven languages, including Greek, Arabic and Japanese, the only one he learned as an adult.

Our generation, that of my brothers and myself, has achieved a deeper level of camouflage: we too belong everywhere and nowhere, but this telltale racial characteristic has been obscured by the chameleon-skin of our new identities. When we left Japan, my father choreographed our reentry into the West: one brother was sent to England, became visibly, audibly English, married an Englishwoman and has two daugh-

3

ters who are anti-Tory and feminist, and would be hard to describe as anything but English. The other brother was sent to America, became ostensibly American, married an American, though he now lives in Italy, and has a son who considers himself more American than Italian. I was sent to Florence and became Italian, to England and became English, to New York and became a New Yorker, if not an American. I am the worst of the chameleons: I have swallowed several ethnic identities whole and no single one lords it over the others. They are all equal and fully developed. I never feel I am translating "myself." There is an "original me" in every language I speak, though this "original" is constantly rendered false by the presence of other, just as original, "originals." And I have to curb my tendency to imitate the accent, dialect, or inflection of the person I am speaking to, and of the country, city, or neighborhood I am in. I sometimes find it hard to distinguish between identity and mimicry. At this rate, it is easy to see that our origins will soon have become invisible.

I come from two versions of the Mediterranean: my mother's family, well, who knows, it has been said that they were pirates who settled in Livorno. There is little evidence to support that, and the name Pinto is, after all, quite common. If this particular strain of Pintos have one thing they share it is lethargy, a quality hardly suited to piracy. Even so, my great-grandfather ended up making a tidy fortune as a cotton merchant in Alexandria. My grandfather, Silvio, vastly increased this fortune in between visits to the Sporting Club, afternoon naps, and secret assignations.

With the help of his partners—relatives, mostly, of which

the youngest was my uncle Aldo—little was left of Pinto Cotton for President Nasser to nationalize. Years later in Milan, Aldo met and married a woman with whom he would, in the course of less than three decades, build a fashion empire, acquire an island in the Caribbean, and houses by the sea, in a forest, in a city, in Italy. Secretly, he dreams of golf and the protracted holiday of retirement.

In Alexandria, my maternal grandmother ran her considerable staff of cooks, parlor maids, gardeners and chauffeurs, and organized afternoon canasta parties for what, even at the time, was an enormous number of people. Our parents had been living in Nairobi while we remained in Alex until the start of the Suez Canal crisis in 1956.

My father's family lived in Rhodes, which was then still an Italian colony, and only left when Mussolini's "racial laws" were passed in 1938. My grandfather was a merchant banker and owned a large portion of the island (which to this day has a street named after him), but still my father, thirteen and the youngest of seven, was barred from attending school. The entire family, except for the eldest son, Jacques, then moved to Alexandria. Jacques was left in charge of the family business and of the family fortune (except for one building belonging to my grandmother that she had, by some premonition, refused to sign over to him). In the years that followed he became increasingly convinced that it was all rightfully his, and ignored my grandfather's repeated requests for funds.

"The world is like a cucumber," says an Arabic proverb my father likes to quote in the original, "sometimes you have it in your mouth and sometimes you have it up your . . ."

So my parents met in Alexandria, in their midteens. She was at the English Girls' School; he was at Victoria College. It was here that their "Englishness" was planted and nurtured. Five years after they met, they decided to get married, or rather, he asked her to marry him, despite the fact that her brother Aldo thought, with characteristic disloyalty towards his nearest and dearest, that my father was throwing himself away, and told him so.

They had a honeymoon by the sea, at Agami, and there the news reached them from Alex that Gino, my mother's brother, had crashed into a farm cart on his way home from a party and died. The photographs show that he was very good-looking in a Leslie Howard sort of way, and there were at least two dozen of his horse-jumping trophies in my grandparents' bedroom. His untimely disappearance conferred on him all perfections. He was barely twenty when he died, my grandmother barely forty-five, but she took to flattening her hair under a hair net and wearing black, grey and lilac. Whatever interest she'd had in society deserted her, which left my grandfather free to make love to an undisclosed number of Alexandrian wives—French, British, Italian. I don't want to make him sound more rakish than he was: behind a Victorian exterior, it was what everybody did, given a chance, and what with the climate, the languor and the natural incestuousness of colonial life, there was no lack of chances.

Neither family was very religious, my mother's even less so than my father's. It is one of the effects of Italy that even people who have been transplanted as often as Jews have, tend to feel Italian before they feel Jewish. And to feel Italian is to feel a little Catholic, after all. Not long after my parents had had their first son, Giampiero, my father decided they should convert to Catholicism. They were in their early twenties then, and one of my father's six brothers, Nissim, who had gone to Rome to study medicine, had been taken by the Germans, first to Auschwitz, then to Buchenwald. For a time, before news reached Alexandria of his whereabouts, no one even knew if he was still alive. It undoubtedly contributed to my father's decision to convert. No member of his family followed the example, except for us, naturally, though we didn't have a choice. Many years later (and by then Nissim had become a prosperous obstetrician in Jamaica Estates, Queens), we learned that none of them approved in the least, no matter what his reasons might have been. But since both of my parents' families were always discreet to the point of being uncommunicative, and certainly as much as possible avoided discussing matters of love, money and religion, I had no idea I was of Jewish descent until I was almost twenty, and came to New York.

In fact, we were brought up as Catholics, which meant that we were baptized, confirmed, and sent to Catholic schools—in Tokyo, they were the only schools for foreigners. When my mother had announced that we were moving from Varese and that we would have to guess where to, we named every city we could think of and had practically given up, till I yelled, "Not Tokyo?" and she nodded. My father had been asked to start a branch of Olivetti, the company that made typewriters and calculators, in Japan. We were given *Il poliglotta inglese*, a very thick book with a Union Jack on the cover whose only appreciable result was that I learned to say *beh-ah-oo-tee-full*. Bribes were offered to make me get through *Little Women* in English, but to no avail: I arrived in Tokyo at the age of ten knowing little more than *shurrupp* and *bye-bye*.

At the Sacred Heart in Tokyo, whose gravel driveway the

feet of boys were not allowed to touch, I wore a white veil and white gloves, sang, "Jesus wants me for a sunbeam," and kneeled in front of a statue of the Virgin Mary reciting, "Oh Mary, I give thee the lily of my heart, be thou its guardian forever," planting a paper lily in a box at her feet. I expect it was our purity we were entrusting to her, and in that sense the prayer differed from an Italian one of later years, "Oh Mary, you who have conceived without sinning, allow us to sin without conceiving." But as far as my father was concerned, being Catholic boiled down to attending Mass on Christmas Eve. Religion was never discussed at home, nor the subject of his conversion. But one family religion that did come with us from country to country was the Mediterranean one of superstition. It was as much a part of our life as the rules of good manners: no walking under ladders, no hats on beds, no open umbrellas in the house, no seating thirteen people at a dinner table, no passing the salt shaker from hand to hand, no pouring wine backhandedly, no crossed handshakes, no toasting with water, no advancing on a street that had been crossed by a black cat, no spilling wine without dabbing it behind the ears, no spilling salt without casting it behind one's shoulders, no lighting more than two cigarettes with one match, no breaking mirrors without throwing the fragments into flowing water, no departures or arrivals on Tuesdays and Fridays. If any of these commandments were unwittingly violated, one had to count to thirteen skipping the even numbers, spit and count backwards, skipping the even numbers, then spit again.

If superstitions took care of what one shouldn't do, proverbs governed the rest. There were sayings accumulated from so many different cultures—Ladino, Italian, French, Turkish, and

Arabic—that it seemed there was one for every situation. "You go to sleep with babies, you wake up wet," that was a Spanish one. "Never too much zeal" was French. "I know my chickens" was Italian. "One day honey, one day onions" was Arabic. It was one of the favorite family games to translate these from the original into a language that would make them sound ridiculous, like this one from the Italian, "So much does the she-cat go to the bacon that she leaves her little paw."

We lived in Alexandria, Cairo and Khartoum, then Tokyo, London and New York. For a time, between Alex and Tokyo, we lived at my grandparents' house in a place called Buguggiate, near Varese in northern Italy. My elder brother, Giampi, was sickly and had been sent to Switzerland with a witchlike governess called Mademoiselle Pourchot who was obsessed with table manners and little else in the realm of human endeavor. My younger brother, Gianchi, and I went to an Italian school in the nearby town of Azzate, where for the first time, in grade school, we studied what was after all meant to be our mother tongue. (In fact, we had already learned Arabic and French, and though the first was soon forgotten for lack of practice, the second is what we spoke at home.) There, in the course of a religion class, the parish priest explained that there were other creeds beside Catholicism, the Moslem one, for instance.

I knew there was something fishy about my grandparents' religion: they never came to Mass with us. That was it, I thought, they must be Moslems. I told the priest very excitedly. He was not only impressed but horrified and stamped home with us to talk to my grandmother. He was told that they were Jewish, not Moslem, and that made it all better, apparently, though it is hard to see why, considering that Islam at least recognizes Christ as a prophet.

There was a defection on my mother's side of the family too: Pierre, a cousin of hers, rose to the rank of monsignor in the Catholic Church. Flying from grand wedding to grand funeral, he has earned himself the honorary title of "Pastor to the Rich and Famous." One faction of the family firmly maintains that he is a spy, and if by that they mean that he is curious, they are right.

Our spinster aunt Nelly preferred Molière and Corneille to the enigmas of theology. Her disheveled mane of bluish hair prompted us to call her Ben-Gurion. She traveled with us from Egypt to Italy, Japan and England, and died peacefully on a plane.

My father's only sister, Sarah, known since her Paris schooldays as *les eaux de Versailles* for her easy tears, decided not to have slipcovers made for her new white couches in Alexandria so that when Nasser confiscated the house and all its contents the couches would be quite filthy. Years later, in Varese, my grandmother, who took pride in her orchard, would say to her, "Aren't these tomatoes good?" and she invariably replied, *"Pas comme en Egypte"* (Not like in Egypt).

I have never gone to Andalusia, where both of my parents' families probably originated and remained until the start of the Inquisition, or to Izmir, where my father's mother was born, or to Rhodes (except once a quarter of a century ago), where Jacques's son still lives with his family, but I did return to Alexandria three times. The first time, ten years ago, I found our house on Abukir Road in Bulkeley unchanged except for

10

the two new office buildings planted on the grounds where the gardens had been. Inside, it was as though my grandparents had moved out the day before. There were still many books on the shelves with my grandmother's name on them. They were probably books she did not feel were "serious" enough to take with her; my grandfather's considerable library is intact, at the house in Varese.

That house now belongs to my uncle Piero, an architect in Milan. It contains whatever furniture and objects my grandparents were able to take with them on the boat from Alex, and many albums of photographs, meticulously labeled and dated. There are images of the houses in Alex, Cairo and Khartoum, of the Sporting Club, of my grandfather with Khadriya Pasha, Farouk's brother-in-law, and other protagonists of these multiple tales.

Finally, Tuscany is where my mother and father and several of his brothers have ended up: the olive groves and vineyards remind them of Rhodes. Mentally, I consider it "home," especially because I live in New York, but it is only one of my "homes" . . .

Strada in Chianti. Olive trees. Rabbits, ducks. Two clouds, one incandescent white, one stormy grey, side by side drawing the shape of a plump baby between them in sky blue, releasing a steady spray of silvery rain on the upraised needled arms of pines and the silvery-leafed olive trees. Theater of flower pots: red hibiscus, pomegranate and geranium, lilac plumbago and lilac, green grapefruit and a lemon tree, a white umbrella, a *hazuk* to open and to shut and to move, as it's held down by two meteorites that fell from the heavens when my father left.

Hazuk is Arabic for the Turkish *kazik,* which is the name of a torture perpetrated with a pole, and a *hazuk* is an awkward thing. That my father left, for instance, might be termed a *hazuk* if it didn't deserve a bigger term. He left and the chaste reign of the little caliph began. The caliph is a brindle-furred houndlet who sleeps on linen sheets—my mother's—and follows her from room to room.

A surrealist painter who drew slices of prosciutto like flags unfurled in the wind made individual portraits of my mother and father—stone-faced, in black cloaks with starched white pleated collars—that would frighten away marauders. They are kept hidden behind the door of what my mother calls "the silly book room" because it contains hundreds of silly books.

The "serious books" are in what used to be my father's study. It was there that he was taken ill one night with a virulent attack of cervical arthritis that made him collapse on one of the two black leather armchairs facing a portrait of Mao Tse-Tung. He had to be covered in blankets, he was shivering so. Does the body signal rebellion before the brain even suspects the enormity of the revolution about to take place? Does shock force pretense to fall away like dead skin? Does the fear of death bring on the fear of not having lived? Does the intensity of illness make one yearn for intensity at large? And do we run away from those who have seen us grappling with our own mortality?

That dizziness was the first taste of the greater dizziness of meeting Cristina and seeing himself reflected in her mirror, her forgiving mirror. He saw finally who he might have been had he not been saddled with the ambitions and morals of the entire Sephardic race, his rabbinical grandfather, stolid father, saintly mother, Victorian upbringing, Anglo-Saxon bias, wife's socially superior family. And I do sympathize: what does our past—his and mine—have to do with our present?

Why should I care about a little island in the Aegean from which he was after all cast off? Why should I have the disadvantages of attachment and roots when I and he have not had their advantages? We have recovered from that past as from every subsequent transient past, from the need for it, God knows from any pride of nationality—what nationality? Greek, Italian, Spanish, Egyptian?—recovered from any religious certainty—he converted because the shame of being Jewish was stronger than any pride of being Jewish and because he did not want to be persecuted for something he did not believe in, as his brother was. He was baptized, took a Christian name, and I was brought up a Catholic because I was not brought up a Jew because as I saw it, and see it still, we considered ourselves primarily free to be anything we wished, so why not Italian, and because my mother freed herself from a past of which she knows nothing and cared nothing, long before us.

Now I see different religions as merely a question of aesthetics—music and architecture—on one hand, and method on the other: how do you become acquainted with the strangers in you? But the more I follow the traces of a "self" that reveals itself as I go, like a path I cannot see, the more I reject every ready-made identity that I or my family might be entitled to, and the very notion of being entitled to any traits that might constrain me from transforming myself into the next "self" that will be as much of an illusion and a delusion as every other.

I feel no connection to the victims in my family, to all they have suffered: I have no pride in their martyrdom—it is not mine. Any faults I have are precisely due to my not having suffered their martyrdoms. Any faults I no longer have are due

13

to my own small martyrdoms, which I take no pride in either, as they made me understand nothing other than savoring the nothing in particular that fills moments. And what the Sephardic Jews suffered was on account of what they were and what they were determined to be, rather than what they weren't. I sympathize, but I wish to open my eyes every day on the possibility of becoming what I am not yet, and of no longer being what I was. As for their languages—Hebrew and Ladino—I don't understand them, don't speak them. I want no family, no religion, no country, no self I have to answer to, please, conform to, die for.

I want to have all the names and lives that every absence of a precedent in me can make room for. I want to belong to nothing other than the secret air that flows through me and bends and colors me. But the chameleon wears a uniform: I am Jewish by race; I was baptized and confirmed a Catholic; I have lived in different countries; I speak some languages; I make a living as a journalist.

Still, this body does not date back to the expulsion of the Jews in 1492, or whenever it was, before or after the Inquisition. It is forty-four years old. It was not conceived in Rhodes, but in Alexandria, by accident—I was born eleven months after my brother—of a father who escaped from Rhodes, from Alexandria, from Italy, from his family's religion, from his family. I resisted the temptation of following his example in escaping from everything and for some years experienced the strangeness of going against myself, of assuming not my identity but my family's—not knowing that there is no such thing.

This body has been in its own places, and bears the mark of those travels. There, it finally forgot what it learned *por boca de madre*. It is the only geography through which I see all others, my only witness and nothing but a vessel of what I still have no idea about.

And yet, who am I trying to fool? I look at a picture of myself and think what Mediterranean features I have after all. A long oval face, long dark hair, brown eyes, a long nose that opens out at the end of the bridge in the shape of a bicycle seat, as my father's does; cabdrivers ask, are you Turkish, are you Indian, are you Spanish? I may have broken with my past but my body hasn't. A woman came up close to me, scrutinizing me as though my skin might yield a label, and asked, "What are you?" I replied, "I am Italian," as I always do, simplifying. "Ah, I knew it," she said triumphantly, "I thought I'd heard an accent," her own accent that of Chief Inspector Clouseau. She said this not thinking perhaps that English is by an overwhelming margin the province of those whose first language it is not.

An Italian friend corrects me, in Italian, on the pronunciation of my vowels, which he considers too "northern" Italian, as though this mouth and throat and tongue of mine, that might once have spoken Aramaic, could adapt endlessly to any pronunciation. That they do, nearly, is what calls attention to the faults: there is no language I speak that is not a mimicry. My accent in every language adapts to the inflections of the person I am talking to, as though the wave of sound from their mouth penetrated my ears and insinuated itself around my vocal cords in spontaneous deference—not mine, my body's. Jews are famous for their powers of adaptation, but famous, too, for wanting to remain among themselves and separate from those who are not them. I want neither, but my body fails me at times.

15

My brother's eldest daughter, Lucie, speaks North London English, which is not the Queen's, and I see her need not to use the constricted music of a constricted class—the upper. Some summers ago, I asked her, "Woy jew spake loik vat?" And she explained, in "proper" English, "If I were to speak the way I'm speaking now at school, everyone would take me for a snob. Besides my boyfriend would think it funny . . ." I don't know how she speaks now, but no doubt, if I am anything to go by, her accent will change many times, until it becomes like mine: imperceptibly "foreign" in every language.

On both sides of the family, an obstacle was dismissed with, "*Ce n'est pas la mer à boire*" (It's not like having to drink the sea), and a dry biscuit was a Christian-choker, *étouffe-chrétien*. If you worried, you were told not to twist your soul into a thread, in Italian, *non farti l'anima a un filo*. Something unremarkable was said to leave the weather it found, in Italian, *lascia il tempo che trova*, or glided on the rails of one's indifference (from Molière). Ornamental objects were called "dust-gatherers," in French *ramasse-poussières*, or *harabish* in Arabic, worthless things, and *halintranke (de puerta)* in Ladino, an odd contraption like the lock on a door. Long after we had left Egypt, the garbage was called *zebala*; a fool was a *homar*, a donkey; how-are-you's were countered with *hamdullellah*, God be praised; a bitch was a *sharmuta*; to be happy was to be *mapsut*; to be light-spirited was to be *hafif*. A show of obstinacy was met with, "*Quand tu as une idée dans la tête, tu ne l'as pas dans les pieds*" (When you have an idea in your head, you don't have it in your feet). And if one pretended not to have heard criticism, one was rebuked with, *"On ne répète pas la messe aux sourds"* (Mass will not be repeated for the deaf).

This book should be in several languages, all the ones spoken by the different members of my family; but I will translate for them as I go along. They translate in their head from one language to another—"switching," as an Alexandrian called it. Among themselves they can speak in a stream whose currents are a number of different languages: in their mouth those tongues become one. English, to record their speech, is as fictional as if a single language had been chosen to record dialogues in the tower of Babel.

I borrowed a little here, a little there, to make a soul for the here and now.

In a furry grey cell at the Museum of Modern Art, sitting on furry steps, I interviewed a young woman for the post of assistant. Her name was Rachel. I was twenty-two. She wasn't sure she wanted the job. She needed to go to Vermont to get her head together, she said. I had been living in England and had never heard the expression, but I said, fine, we could talk again. We got up. She walked to the elevator. I could see her standing in profile. The doors of the elevator opened, and suddenly, she turned on her heels, walked back towards me, right up to me, her mouth at the height of my throat, and said, "Excuse me, but are you a Sephardic Jew?" I was conscious of a feverish sensation in the brain, as though messengers in sharp heels were running to and fro, tying loose ends of information together. I said "No," immediately, then "I don't know," then "Yes, maybe." She left. I sat down. What? Of course: they spoke that funny Spanish among themselves, didn't they? And the name wasn't Italian. It seems incredible that I didn't know but it was such an obvious thing, so enormous, I would have known it if it had been true so the fact I didn't excluded it from my realm of conjecture, from my thoughts altogether.

The alleged Princess Anastasia Romanov, in her nineties and living in Virginia somewhere, when asked by a reporter to say something that would prove beyond a doubt who she was, replied, "Could you say anything to prove who *you* are?" What one is is only a matter of memory, and if parents "forget," the secret stays secret. I don't think they did it intentionally, but I don't recall that they ever pronounced the words "Jewish" and "Sephardic," either separately or together; besides after the age of fifteen I saw them once or twice a year, and they spent every moment we had getting me to toe the line, stay in my frescoed prison like a good girl, not smoke, study hard. At the boarding school of Poggio Imperiale, I wasn't sitting beneath a portrait of our blessed foundress Maria Carolina of Saxony, wondering, Jewish or not Jewish, Sephardic or Ashkenazi. I was reciting, "Hail Mary, full of grace, the Lord is with thee . . . ," as I had been taught.

Even now, the closest I've come to a rabbi was a travel agent specializing in cheap fares; if I asked for a ticket to Milan, he would say, "Voy not Tel Aviv? I gechoo goot kreis." One could only fly Pan Am, never on Friday or Saturday, and one had to be careful to not even graze his sleeve, or he would scuttle sideways like a threatened porcupine. "Hi, Joe," stewardesses cajoled when he entered the VIP lounge with me a few steps

18

behind. "You vont a grink?" he'd say. "Havvah grink!" Once, he got me a ticket that made me out to be a Mrs. Rosenberg who had been to New York and was on her way back to Manchester and I thought that if the plane fell, no one would know I was on it. There was one other rabbi, at one of two synagogues I've been in, where a cousin had his bar mitzvah. I was in the ladies' room, fiddling with my camera. When I emerged, the rabbi, said, "You're not supposed to put lights on on the Sabbath." "What lights?" I asked. I wasn't even using a flash.

Walking back from the park, I become curious about the cement building on Fifth Avenue and Sixty-fifth Street, called Temple Emanu-El. It is so tall, and placed so right against the street, that it is difficult to perceive it as anything but a blank endless wall. I look up, see the façade, the sign saying "Meditation and Prayer . . . entrance on 65th Street." I go and see what it is like inside: the same mammoth, dwarfing proportions as the Metropolitan Opera. Here, too, a giraffe could stand, stretch its neck. Gold, turquoise, crimson mosaics. Five different hues of marble. The American flag. Hundreds of polished, upholstered pews. What do I feel? Nothing. What am I thinking of? Of Jesus overturning the merchants' stalls inside the temple. I recite a Buddhist prayer. At home, I listen to Vespers of the Annunciation. I can't help the cocktail of infidelities.

It is comforting to think that there is *someone* who can help: for a long time that was what religion meant to me. When I still believed that I began and ended where I could see and understand, and saw myself as finite, I was afraid of my own shadow. How could I, if I was only this physical body and this brain, know anything of any use in the face of fear?

Of course, I don't remember being baptized, but I was, in Alexandria, shortly after my birth at the Benito Mussolini Italian Hospital presided over by my great-uncle Carlo, an obstetrician, and I don't expect that any other member of my family on my mother's or my father's side attended, Jewish as they still were, and are.

In Azzate, my brother Gianchi and I, after a suitable course in catechism, received our First Communion: he wore a pale grey suit and a white sash around his arm, and I a bride's white dress and veil. There is a photograph of me in profile, my tongue eagerly stretched towards the first taste of Christ in a wafer. It glued itself against my palate, then and every subsequent time I took Communion, and had to be pried away by a labor of the tongue. Wearing the same outfits, we were confirmed at the church in Varese by a slap on the cheek from the Cardinal of Milan, Montini, who later became Pope Paul VI, so it was a privileged slap.

A certain Gaston Piha on my grandmother Berthe's side took a trip around the world, and in India, wishing to gain admittance to a Buddhist temple, converted to Buddhism. Years went by, he was married and widowed. One day, he decided to remarry—a Frenchwoman and a Catholic. The parish priest of Santa Caterina in Alexandria asked him what religion he belonged to, and he replied, "I am a Buddhist!" The priest was puzzled. "What is this Buddhist religion?" Gaston explained that he had converted to Buddhism many years before, but that he was Jewish by birth. The priest was relieved. "Oh, an Israelite, now that's a more Christian religion!" and proceeded to convert him.

When he was almost a year old, my uncle Aldo came down with gastroenteritis: he had a nanny from Friuli named Elda who had allowed him to eat fresh dates. His temperature rose horribly. The doctor came twice a day. One evening it seemed Aldo would die, but he was revived by an injection. Still, his condition worsened again to such a degree that the doctor took my grandfather aside and told him to prepare his wife as the case was desperate. The cook Lucia, who was very pious, persuaded my grandmother to light a candle to the Madonna. A friend sent a rabbi, to whom my grandfather gave a small donation. Next came my great-grandparents' servant, Mohammed, who swore by his Moslem guru, Sidi 'el Morghani, a Berber like himself; to him also my grandfather gave a donation. When the doctor returned from dinner, he held Aldo's wrist for a few seconds, then exclaimed, "This is a miracle, he is out of danger." From then on, Aldo was known as the miracle boy, though no one could say to whom he owed the miracle.

My brother Giampi had his First Communion in Cairo and on that occasion was given a little wooden Madonna with a halo. He took her with him wherever he went. In Alexandria he kept her on a wooden cabinet, along with other cherished possessions. He noticed that every time the family doctor came, the Madonna was spirited away so that he wouldn't see it and report it to our grandmother Rebecca, who was supposed to know nothing of our conversion.

She took Giampi to see the windows of the most elegant department store in Alexandria, called Hannaux. At Christmas, there was a decorated tree and Rebecca commented to him,

"See what the pagans have wrought!" Giampi was six and had already noticed that if we were in our flat in Cairo there would be a tree at Christmas, but if we were in Alexandria there wouldn't be.

In Tokyo, on my first day of school at the Sacred Heart, a Belgian nun in a wheelchair, Mother Lemmon, was wheeled out of retirement to ask me a question in French, since I did not yet understand English. She had a short white stubble on her chin from occasional shaving, and the folds of her face were enveloped in the crinkly white blinders of her order. The black veil flowed down from the top of her head in a pyramid shape, and as I write this it occurs to me that all nuns have something of the sphinx: they are allowed to keep their private life a secret. Like all the sisters at Sacred Heart, she wore a pleated black habit, with a black rosary hanging from the belt and vanishing into a seam pocket. Her eyes were pale blue jellied over with cataracts. Her question was, *"Voulez-vous vous communier?"* and though I knew I was being asked whether I wanted to take Communion, I was struck by the awkwardness of her French. I replied I did not.

The reason they wished to pry into something that even the Church considers to be a matter between the individual and his God was that two separate lines had to be formed to walk to Mass every Friday. Those who took Communion sat in the front pews, and so filed into the chapel from a separate entrance—a form of spiritual segregation. The lines would form on either side of the long wood-paneled corridors of the hybrid neoclassical building that was our school. On the walls were large signs, black on white, at regular intervals, that ordered,

SILENCE—we were not allowed to talk in the files, a rule we loved to break. The floor was of mottled marble, the kind that seems to have been spat by a giant who has been chewing multicolored rocks. A line five inches wide had been drawn in white marble.

For Mass, we wore white nylon gloves and a tulle veil that had an elastic sewn onto the underside of it, which, slipped over our heads and behind our ears, would hold it down. There was a time when I was cast into transports of devotion at Mass. I prayed with my eyes shut and hoped one nun or another would notice my fervor. What I was hoping to achieve I don't know, but there was enough admiring talk of martyrs for me to want to be one. I watched in envy as schoolmates broke an arm and had to have it in a plaster cast, or hurt an eye and wore a black patch over it. I saw their injuries as distinctions and as opportunities to demonstrate bravery. One girl, in an accident, had both of her legs broken. She was put in a cast that went from her waist to her ankles, like a mummy, and a handle was attached across her stomach so that she could be carried. This, I thought, must be heaven.

The only three-day retreat I attended at the school, sleeping in a grey cell, was distinguished by the readings we were entertained with at lunchtime. We were made to vow not to speak for three days. And so, to fill the void of our silence while we ate and make it easier for us to resist talking, a nun would read to us from the lives of saints. It was the life, or rather, death, of Saint Eulalia that impressed itself on my memory as I ate my chicken stew: " . . . her tender sides were torn with iron hooks, lighted torches were applied to her breasts . . . instead of groans, nothing was heard from her mouth but thanksgivings. The fire, at length catching her hair, surrounded her head and

23

face and the saint was stifled by the smoke and flame . . . a white dove was seen to come out of her mouth and to wing its way upwards when the holy martyr expired . . . pilgrims came to venerate her bones . . ." In retrospect, this was a Catholic lesson in equanimity: as the martyr is tortured and killed, you continue to swallow your little meal.

We were made to say prayers before and after every class in spite of the fact that the Christians were not a majority. Mass lasted about an hour, except on special feast days, when it lasted, it seemed to me, an eternity—a foretaste of the purgatory of boredom. When I was about eleven I was taught a song I couldn't stop singing for several months:

Jesus wants me for a sunbeam,
at home, at school, at play,
in every way I try to please Him,
at home, at school, at play.

A sunbeam, a sunbeam,
Jesus wants me for a sunbeam,
a sunbeam, a sunbeam,
I'll be a sunbeam for Him.

This went on until I discovered *The Tales of Hoffman* and started humming, "Oh Hoffman's made you a victim of his brutal desires, only your beauty he admires . . ."

My elder brother would dare Gianchi to have an orgasm sitting at the long black crystal table in the dining room—a remnant of the German embassy that had once been there—with all the guests around him and nothing but a distended little smile to indicate he had won the bet. Gianchi was keeper of the secret of eros. Our second house in Tokyo was a sprawling low brick building all on one floor, except for my brothers' room, which was up three steps. There, past the lion skin—my pants often got caught on one of the teeth in its shellacked, eternally roaring mouth—I found Gianchi, on the bed with a postcard-sized television on his stomach, watching samurai films, which is how he learned to say "*Narukodo,*" in a low pensive voice, which means "Indeed." Shoguns said it to gain time. I sat on the side of the bed, and tried to infiltrate his symbiosis with the television screen. How is it done? I asked. The man puts his thing in. What? Nooooo—how can it point upwards when it points downwards? *Boh.* I had seen one in Varese, years earlier, and it had looked to me like a toad: the head, the haunches, the delicate creased skin like the lid of a sleepy eye. Candido, our gardener in Varese, seemed to be coaxing it as though to stand on its hind legs and crane its neck. He had caught me in the cottage by the gate where my parents lived, separated by a little hill, a big chestnut tree, a bed of dahlias, from the main house where we lived with our grandparents. I was opening bottles in the bathroom, sniffing their contents, smoothing my mother's creams on my cheeks—Velva by Elizabeth Arden . . . The samurai skipped from a roof, across a pond, onto a hillock, and brandished the sword at his opponent. Okay, then what? Nothing. Nothing? Nothing. I saw sex, after that conference, as a union of immobilities. It was a book by Giorgio Bassani, *Behind the Door*, in which a boy looking through a keyhole sees a couple making love, that revealed to me that there was movement, too. I knew what an orgasm was but I didn't know anyone else did, that it had a name, or that it had anything to do with what I thought of as "sex"—an amorous sea into which one could sink and stay with the right person, kiss, and kissing too I saw as a still conjunction. I was raised a Catholic. I learned to confess to "impure thoughts," felt filthy thinking them, waited for love to cast a benediction over my life and cut the ribbon of its beginning. *Narukodo.*

Just as my brothers and I were becoming unbearably ourselves, we were sent away to three different countries: Giampi to Britain, Gianchi to America, I to Italy. Our parents stayed in Japan. My father went to "the office"—that magical and secret container of everything sanctified as duty. My mother practiced *sumi-e* brushstrokes and he went on business trips to Nagoya, Osaka, Yokohama, Fukuoka—like women's names, they all ended in *a*. The separation was thought necessary "for us," but also for him—so he could continue his life as a young man, or rather resume it where he had left off, before we came into existence.

One sign of my father having gone to Victoria College in Alexandria, from the age of fifteen on, was that he only wore English shoes and because his right foot was deformed, he had them custom-made in London. All his shoes looked alike—brogues and half-brogues, black or brown. But he could differentiate between them: a finer, shinier leather for evening, suede and coarse reddish leather and a thicker sole for weekends, plain black for the daytime. The number of holes also indicated a range of codes from the elegant to the casual: the more holes there were the sportier the shoe.

The tacit puritanical dictum was that one should always appear to be wearing the same shoes, that one didn't spend either one's time or money on anything so frivolous. If I have followed any sartorial model, it is my father's rather than my mother's: uniformity that renders variety invisible to all but the wearer, who alone wallows in the pleasure of a new jacket, without having to withstand the scrutiny of others. The only "loud" thing he ever wore was a checked jacket, on weekends, in tones of yellow, orange, mustard, green. Argyle socks always accompanied this flamboyance.

The first sign of another woman in his life was a belt he wore one day: it was of woven fabric mounted on leather depicting ducks flying eagerly towards the buckle. On his customary grey worsted suit, made to order in Hong Kong or Torino, with the usual brogues, white shirt, three-quarter socks, the belt spoke volumes. Later signs of liberation from his imaginary status as a British subject: more and more pairs of American shoes; windbreakers in the place of the usual blue or camel cashmere coats; pajamas with short pants.

When my parents left a bathroom, the toothbrush was in the glass, the cap on the tube of toothpaste had been replaced. I never saw a pair of knickers on the floor, clothes on a chair. All evidence of daily life was quickly effaced. The only transgressions in their existence ruled by cleanliness and neatness were provided by the dogs: hair everywhere, sprinklings of urine on bedspreads and couches, drool.

For they are Wasp-like Jews. They discussed their feet with a degree of pride not accorded to any of their other traits, physical or intellectual. They do what they do without any apparent concern for tactics, strategy, artifice—all thought to be supremely vulgar if *consciously* exercised. It was understood that one did not talk about clothes, possessions, money or even food, unless absolutely unavoidable. The only two areas that allowed them some freedom were their dogs, for outbursts of emotion, and their feet, for expressions of self-worth and, make no mistake about it, superiority.

Pretending to be talking about their feet, they could say just how much better they thought they were: No one has feet like these; and, it's not easy to have pretty feet; and, have you ever seen such fine, regular toes; and, were there ever toes that were less marked by the constriction of shoes? etc. They would lie on the bed, sometimes, during a siesta, and compare their feet. This was the only instance, too, where they openly competed and my mother did not yield. My father would say, "Don't look at my right foot"—for that one had been deformed by a bout of meningitis in childhood—"look at the perfection of my left foot." And my mother countered, "But look at mine, so delicate . . ." This invariably ended with him conceding that her feet looked better on her than his would. It was, I suspect, their talk of love. ("Believe it or not," my mother said when she read this, "there was talk of love, too—he would hug me at night and say, 'Never, never leave me,' or 'What would I do if you died before me?' ")

As for expressing their feelings towards others, they never did so with the abandon and unmitigated partiality that they showed the dogs—whatever dogs happened to be around at any given time, a minimum of one to a maximum of three. They were hugged, kissed, stroked, petted, talked to in baby voices, for every time any one of us, including my mother and father, wasn't.

My parents discussed their dogs the way others discuss their children. "Larry is very shy, poor thing, he hasn't yet re-

28

covered from the initial trauma of being kept in a low kennel for such a long time. But I think you are beginning to trust me now, Larry, aren't you? You know that if it hadn't been for me, you might still be there," my father would say, repeatedly kissing the miniature wirehaired dachshund on the muzzle and pulling on its paws as he held it cradled against his chest. Myron, the basset hound, had only to look soulful, which he did very easily, for them to start speculating he might be nostalgic for his first home in Germany. He also liked, having observed the presence of a visitor, to enter a room demurely and pee on the man's leg, for he did this only to men; there was no question whose side my parents would be on: "Myron was disturbed by the arrival of a stranger in the house, poor thing . . ." Papaya, a dachshund who wrapped his paws around every new woman's legs and became so aroused that the strawberry tip of his penis would protrude as he rhythmically thrust his pelvis back and forth with a look of rapt abandon in his eyes, was said to be "the most intelligent son of a bitch."

There was Chianti, a model of chivalry and kindheartedness; Dindo the Dalmatian—also known as Bhopal, for the toxic clouds he emitted from the pink creases of his bottom. All slept on their bed, sat on sofas, ate at their table. They were discussed tenderly, in a low voice. Every morning they were fed squares of buttered toast sprinkled with salt, because Tuscan bread is unsalted, and since this is something my mother likes to do she assumes the dogs share her tastes. Every evening, they would line up by the little chest next to my father's side of the bed; it contained a tin labeled "Good Boy Choc Drops." My father distributed the flat round pastilles gingerly, like a priest dispensing Communion. The number of pastilles never varied, and each dog received the same amount, as my father firmly believed that our dogs could appreciate a climate of supreme justice, or at any rate be offended by the least sign of favoritism. Now that my father has left home, this last ritual has been abolished, also because it proved ruinous: the Dalmatian—considered an albino—died prematurely of hepatic cirrhosis.

My father's place in the matrimonial bed is now being warmed, though partially, by the new dachshund, Vasco, who lies splayed on the white cotton crochet bedspread at night, his black head resting on a candid white linen pillow case. It would be extreme to say that he is the new master of the house, but there is no question that he has at least mitigated my mother's grief at my father's departure.

He eats spaghetti, barks at animals on television, and digs up roots of plants in the garden. He takes it upon himself, too, to make guests welcome by lavishing attentions on them when they come down for breakfast in the morning, and greeting them, every time they reappear on the scene, as though he had not lived in their absence, with strangled squeals, sinuous writhing, feverish wagging. It is not my father's outstretched hand and enamored green eyes beneath bushy brows, but it will do.

All the dogs that died at Strada in Chianti are buried in the garden there, between the pines and the vineyard. There is a large rock to mark the spot and on it have been affixed terracotta plates for each departed dog—especially made in nearby Impruneta—with names and dates.

How important is the matter of race if dogs have been some of the most venerated members of our family? If we, my parents, my brothers and I, are purebred Sephardic Jews, they, most certainly, are not. Vasco, my mother's best-loved dog, was

30

originally named Marko and came from Germany; he is even a von Something, and my mother, before falling for him completely, referred to him as "the Deutsch mark." Vasco was also my father's nickname for her, because like the explorer, she has a sense of direction.

"As my father used to say," my father tells me on the telephone, "there are times when everything comes up in the shape of a horn." Between words, he whispers to a secretary, "Please leave a copy of this on my desk," and "Thank you." He says he is going to Japan to "see" about a "thing" that could be interesting. "Is Cristina going with you?" I ask. "No, no," he replies quickly to the suggestion that amusement might be on the horizon, "this is strictly business." "Have you spoken to my mother?" I ask. "Yes, call her in Paxos, it will make her happy. She is swimming and working. She is much better, I think," he replies as one speaking of a patient.

"The patient" is in fact a good name for my mother, as patience has distinguished her forty-five years of dedicated service to the institution of marriage. "Nora," my father would order as soon as she opened one eye in the morning, "take a piece of paper and write." (This proved prophetic eventually as in the after-him she has written several cookbooks.) He would dictate a list of guests to be invited to dinner, the menu, letters to be sent. "We should invite Fiore to dinner," he would say, "the poor thing, he is all alone." In Tokyo, there was an endless stream of "poor things"— people stranded far from home, without family or friends, in a city that was then impenetrable to foreigners. "At the Meiji ice-cream billboard, turn left," guests were told. Formal dinner invitations were accompanied by a

31

little mimeographed map of the area and arrows indicating the route to be taken.

"Poor things" have besieged our existence, since, in case you had not understood, it was my father who decided everything, except what we thought. "Poor things" encountered in Sydney, Osaka, Cape Town, appeared on our doorstep in Chianti, with their entire family. "Take them to Florence and show them the city," my father would tell the patient, "the poor things don't speak the language." The other poor thing, my mother, followed his orders to the letter.

Of course my mother was not patient at all, only obedient. She seethed serenely, inconspicuously, clandestinely, behind her own back, for almost five decades. The tension of resentment lurked beneath her every gesture. It was ascribed to the Pinto character. To be short-tempered, bossy, or willful was "very Pinto." To be unnaturally considerate, to have big hands, to make jokes, was "very Alhadeff," and to make these distinctions was also very Alhadeff. It was presumed that to be an Alhadeff was better than being anything else, certainly better than being a Pinto.

There is the not irrelevant question of size: the Pintos are small, the Alhadeffs are big. The Pintos believe that do-goodering should begin and end at home; the Alhadeffs see the world at large as their mission. The Pintos follow their instincts, the Alhadeffs their morals. I needn't tell you that the former appear somewhat selfish while the latter appear heroic. But the selfish are true to themselves while the heroic often are not and at some point in their existence find the pretense intolerable and cast the whole bloody lot off to become the other face of the coin. Coins enter into this story, as one half of my father's family were bankers. The other half were rabbis. Preachiness regarding money matters was the traditional cause of dissension between my father and myself.

An example of the heroic and the selfish? The "poor thing" mentioned earlier would come to dinner; my mother would, against her will, carefully prepare it, or have it prepared by our housekeeper, Emiko-san, and my father would reap the benefit of a gesture that generously disposed of someone else's time.

I breathed all this in and it molded every cell in my body, put down every trace of every plan I blindly followed till I began to see that there were at least two people inside me, one of whom proceeds straight from a father who built those around him in his image and a mother who built herself and those around her in his; the other I discover now.

"This *damn* country," my mother would say of Japan when its ways, which weren't hers, tried her patience too far. She was the unalterable foreigner whose task it was to reject difference at the very moment when even he, for all his enthusiasm and sympathy for Japan, could no longer bear it.

Her version of an evening at the Kabuki: the Japanese "crying like calves" at the truculent plots being enacted, and all the while chewing dried fish. Of the strangled cries of the actors, so moving to others, she said, "One more of those and I leave." Leave they did. Very likely my father was relieved not to have to test the limits of his own endurance.

When she lost her temper and raised her voice, he would whisper infuriatingly to her, "*Don't* shout, you know they never shout here." This always made the tension escalate. It stirred up the fundamental problem: he treated her as a slightly inferior being who could not understand *certain* things because she was prosaic, and he, infinitely tolerant, had to be patient in his attempt to redeem her. But I suspect that even in being what he wished she wasn't she was exactly as he wished her to be—expressing what he was too high-minded to express.

At the much mythicized tea ceremony, my mother resented all that made it mythical—the slow twisting and turning of the bowl this way and that, the deliberate whisking of the liquid, three circles to the left, three circles to the right, the silence, the pauses, the livid suspense, and all to obtain a "bitter thick green stuff with that disgusting foam on top." Not to mention the "sticky, tasteless" bean-paste sweets served with it.

Hers is not a contemplative nature and she would never accept a connection between her meticulous crochet work—320 squares to every bedspread—the just as meticulous completion of two full books of crossword puzzles a week, and contemplation. Once when she was persuaded to try yoga, she assumed the required position, then said, "Now what?"

She has a horror of healthy things: hot broths, cereals, low salt and low sugar, vegetarianism. When people talk about Milan being polluted, she dismisses it as facetious. Short of one's being at death's door, she does not consider illnesses worth thinking about; she does not consider most ailments even illnesses. She believes that vitamins are rubbish and that there is nothing wrong with pesticides and chemicals in general. She venerates plastic: "Tupperware," plastic glasses and dishes, "for the garden," which are not disposable (that would be an advantage) but, she maintains, lighter to carry. She loves the dishwasher to the point that she'll juggle things around endlessly until everything fits, even though it would have taken less time to wash the nonfitting item by hand. Before setting out on a car journey, she plots the course carefully: she'll choose a dirt road any time over the speedway if it's shorter in kilometers, no matter how ugly, no matter the lack of urgency.

She does not like anything, or anyone, at the last minute. The only thing she likes to do on the spur of the moment is what she had planned to do, and if that's nothing, then nothing it is. She has no aptitude at all for making herself appear as interesting as she is: at a first, even second or third glance, very little is revealed of her exotic past. She likes to be thought perfectly normal as opposed to extraordinary or idiosyncratic. If she captures the fancy of others it is for lack of trying. There is an aristocratic streak in this willful combination of doing nothing to please and assuming one will anyway. That is, as far as the outside world is concerned. Till recently, it was something she could afford to do because my father was her entire universe, and frankly she did not need anyone else.

II

Most families believe that they are endowed with extraordinary powers or gifts, or at least they long for proof of this: that others are common while they are exceptional. Secretly, of course, they think anyone is better than they are. But who is not hampered by the body that blocks progression every step of the way between heaven and earth? It is the body that fabricates desire and desire is responsible for the idea of religion, and of nation.

My families are no different from most. On my mother's side, on my father's side, they believe they are superior. My mother's believed they were better bred than my father's, and my maternal grandmother's believed they were better bred than her husband's, on and on, no doubt all the way back to the apes, when there must have been a noble ape and a common ape before they were all just hairy beasts who walked on all fours.

All the same, my own cousin Pierre sat on my couch and told me that Alexandria owed its "atmosphere" to six or seven families and that though my grandmother Berthe was welcomed into this group my grandfather Silvio was not, and, I was relieved to hear, neither were "Larry" Durrell until he married Claude of the elect ("but by that time Alexandria was finished"), nor Cavafy who smoothed my cousin's hair once when he was a child.

What would those six families have been, what would that famous Atmosphere have been, even before attempting the controversial task of drawing in a few other Sephardic Jewish families, without their servants—Egyptian, Greek, Yugoslav, Italian—who polished, dusted, nourished, gardened, changed the sheets of the Atmosphere? Not to mention the non-Atmosphere that crowded the streets, manned the Sporting Club, lay destitute at its gates waiting for tips. They were on a very long waiting list inhabited by imperceptible shades of the grey well-to-do, to the not well-to-do, to the nothing-doing, all-hankering, the latter for anything from subsistence to shining luxury. And whoever reached this exalted level must have known that outside of that Atmosphere, other cities were inhabited by their own impenetrable Atmosphere.

Snobbism is an animal that can always find something to feed on. One lofty Atmospherina, Madame S., Pierre recounts, was looking to invite Queen Geraldine of Albania (an Ester-hazy) to dinner. As the telephone numbers were often changed for security reasons, Madame X called Madame B., also of the A., to obtain the new telephone number. It was the nanny, Miss Stone, non-Atmospheric but instrumental in not letting soiled air penetrate the A., who looked into the address book. "I have it in my hands," she said, "I'm looking through it, let's see . . . Q . . . Q . . . Q . . . *Queens*: Elena, Frederica, Giovanna, oh *here* she is, Geraldine." "That's Alexandria in the forties," Pierre says. "The queens *ne fréquentaient pas la maison* Pinto"—Silvio and Berthe—he adds. It is clear that anyone who has to ask a nanny for the phone number is not an insider. I put it to you that Madame X waited for her friend to go out so she could find the nanny alone. And anyone who has a listing for "Queens" in their address book is a snob.

Pierre abandoned Alexandria at the age of nineteen and some ten years later, bypassed the problem of social standing altogether by working directly for God. He was ordained a priest.

You call at some aristocrat's house in Rome: Pierre is arriving by train, at six. A message is left for him with the woman who answers in a slightly foreign accent. Nonetheless, you call before he has a chance to. You know that if you want to see him, you had better catch him before he makes his three or four different appointments for the evening. He has just walked in. Will he come to dinner at . . . Actually he had a plan to see . . . , but . . . Where? he wants to know. At Nino's, you say, on the Via Borgognona. He will see what he can do, and call back in ten minutes. Does so in three: "See you there at nine-thirty."

He is there when we arrive, wearing a shirt of impalpable grey poplin with the edge of the collar sewn down revealing two inches of the white plastic strip of priesthood he normally keeps in a breast pocket and slips on if the occasion calls for it. In restaurants, he says, it gets him better service. He orders like one who does not always eat what, or as much as, he would like to: grilled porcini mushrooms, grilled steak and beans, and he'll relinquish a piece of his mushrooms for a taste of your fried brains.

He cultivates writers and artists, has adopted them as his flock. In New York I had introduced him to the photographer Robert

Mapplethorpe. Robert called me to say, "I played footsie with your cousin under the table."

Pierre told me the story of one writer, Giorgio Manganelli, who called and begged him to come see him as soon as possible. Pierre replied that he had some appointments but could be there in the afternoon. The man insisted he try to get there earlier. Pierre said, "I arrived on time for our appointment and he was dead," and laughed as though trying to cast off a guilty conscience, or as though it didn't matter. He officiated at the man's funeral and at that of Pier Vittorio Tondelli, another writer, who died of AIDS.

There was a young sculptor from New Zealand who lived with him for a time, at his "lemon grove" by Lake Garda. He had secured for him a large studio with a view on the top floor of a building belonging to the carabinieri, and an exhibition in a gallery in Milan. When he left, Pierre said, "He is a New Zealander, he has to be in New Zealand," then added, "I miss him because he used to wash my dishes, I hate washing dishes, anyone who stays at my house has to do it." Now he has "my Trappist," of whom he says, "I'm sure he is a masochist: whenever I ask him to do something, like weeding the garden, he does it quickly and thoroughly." The Trappist reads Homer over and over, and Stendhal—"no trash like this," Pierre said, indicating a biography of Capote he had been immersed in—"I know all the people in it, you see." But the Trappist can't drive, something a young writer he was recently introduced to might be able to do.

Pierre officially retired some time ago but he still hasn't done so. He co-officiates at Mass every day in Gargnano, except if one of the parish priests in his area asks to be substituted for one or two days. He will now be receiving, for his services to the Church, a monthly pension of less than five hundred dollars. "How will I live?" he mused. "Well, at least, I pay no rent, my friends buy me clothes . . ." They provide him with airline tickets when he needs one or they need him; international calling cards; a credit card for emergencies; a budget to buy exhibition catalogues and go to the theater. Still, he admitted, "it's hard sometimes, having to rely on others for everything I need." I tried to console him, saying it was probably easier on the giver. "Not for *me* it isn't," he retorted vehemently. Then, in a mixture of sheepishness and pride: "Now I will tell you something I never told anyone before. There is a woman, near where I live, she is now thirty-five, who has been in love with me for years. I only speak to her on the telephone: I've told her I will not see her. Every now and then, she leaves something for me at my house, when I'm not there: a new T-shirt, a pair of pants, this shirt I'm wearing."

If you say, "Nice bathing suit," he'll say he hasn't bought one since 1934 and that he gets them from one friend who gives him the ones he's worn for six years. One aristocratic benefactor, who is very tall, gives him clothes, and so does his brother, who is very short, and both fit him perfectly: "It's lucky that I seem to be made of rubber: everything looks good on me."

Pierre's *r*'s are neither French nor Italian. He absorbs attention like a child. He drops names the way certain women put on too many jewels (for which he has a predilection): "I have to go and see Burroughs, I promised . . . I am having dinner with Lou Reed . . . Gus Van Sant was there . . . the Queen and Prince Philip were at the wedding—I was invited but I declined . . . " Months later: "I've just returned from Lawrence, Kansas, where Burroughs taught me to shoot. We went out to a field and set up targets. We had three or four guns. Mine was a Colt .45, a very nice object to hold in your hand, like a nice walking stick. I didn't know you had to hold your left hand under your right when you shoot—" he demonstrated "—like this."

He throws out subjects of conversation like a jukebox display that stops when a selection is made: he stops when one shows interest. He gives no space to silence when he is in company, though one imagines he must spend much of his life steeped in it. He never talks about that, or about being a priest much, except when the situation—a person's plight, whether clear or below the surface—calls for the kindness of a priest. Then, a quiet unassuming halo is deployed.

It was when he was at Cambridge that he claims he realized he would have to make a choice between being a playboy or becoming a priest: both require a proclivity for promiscuity, and time—the only thing one can give to people who suffer, since they need nothing but the illusion, now and then, that they are not alone.

Wherever he goes, he introduces himself to the local parish priest and offers to relieve him of saying one of the daily Masses. He arrived once in Strada in Chianti and, at the Church of Santa Cristina, Don Camillo was celebrating the commemoration of Christ washing the feet of the disciples before the Last Supper. Pierre offered to "con-celebrate" Mass with Don Camillo. Twelve men volunteered to stand in as disciples, among them Vasco, the shepherd, and Pierfrancesco, the butcher. They sat on a bench that had been placed against the wall, to the right of the altar. In the middle of Mass, the men removed the shoe and sock from their right foot. Don

41

Camillo came down from the altar bearing a white enamel basin with a blue border, filled with water. He knelt at the feet of each of the men: first he sprinkled a little water from the basin on the naked foot, then he patted it dry with a linen towel he had draped over one arm. The men looked sheepish, as though caught doing something obscene. Pierre sat in a corner and repeated the lines of the accompanying text.

In August, he takes over a parish on the outskirts of Rome, so the local priest can take a holiday. It is grim work because he is only called on to minister to the dead or dying. "At least," he remarked cheerfully, "funerals are always unexpected." Anyone wanting to get married or baptized waits for their priest to return. Still, the parish is not far from the beach, and though "squalid," has "lovely terraces."

I heard him say once that though he does not set much store by the Virgin Mary, he believes in the Holy Spirit. His explanation of the Eucharist is: "When you are in love, you want to 'eat' your love, you want total union . . . When we were young, we were told that we should not touch the host with our teeth, but I do: I eat it voluptuously. Christ said: 'Eat my body.' "

His problem as a priest, he says, vis à vis Church and critics, is his optimism, often interpreted as superficiality. "I have not the least doubt," he says, "that we are already saved and that we are already experiencing eternal life. Every act of love and every feeling of love is a model of the afterlife. Saint John tells us so in his first letter." He believes in love as much as he believes in God, or in both inseparably: "I think that Paradise is like being in love and love being reciprocated . . . plus the certainty that this condition will never end, which is particularly pleasant. "

At the house in Chianti, I heard the bell, then the sound of the gate opening. I told a friend on the telephone, "Guess who's just arrived?" "Who?" "Pierre." I continued to talk on the phone but moved over to the window so as to observe the arrival. He emerged from a brand-new grey-green Fiat Uno (later he explained it was "catalytic," meaning that it used "green gasoline"—the nonpolluting kind—and I assumed that one of his benefactors had given it to him as a present), bearing a wooden crate half filled with peaches. I yelled hello and asked him to come upstairs so he could speak to our mutual friend. He made his way up the stairs, peaches and all, found me in my mother's bedroom, took the receiver from my hands, reclined on the freshly made bed diagonally, his head on the white linen pillows. Elegant as ever: he wore a canary yellow polo shirt, uncreased baggy navy-blue cotton pants and rubber thong sandals with a thick sole and blue synthetic velvet straps. He is balding but still has a few strands he keeps very long so they cover the top of his head; he has long thin legs and arms, beautiful long hands, the hint of a tan, small features, grey-blue eyes.

I heard my mother having a fit and went into the study where she was. "I will not pay another fine," she blurted, "it's not fair, the carabinieri probably came here, saw the house and decided I could pay another fine, but I won't pay it. I'm going over there right now . . . This *bloody* country."

"What fine?" I asked.

"One hundred thousand lira 'for driving too fast, given the

conditions of the road,' and that's on top of the two hundred for driving with an expired license." I tried to calm her and to tell her not to appear angry in front of the carabinieri. She promised halfheartedly, saying, "I must go now," and swept down the stairs and into the car. She barely acknowledged Pierre but he didn't seem to mind. When I too got off the phone, I found him alone, in the living room, reading the *Corriere della Sera*.

As I went up to him to give him a kiss, he said, "I smell, I didn't wash." I noticed that he hadn't shaved. Then he confided, settling deeper into the couch, "I have to pee. Remind me to pee."

"Go and pee," I said promptly. "The bathroom is very close."

"Well, not now," he demurred.

I went into the kitchen to start taking the dishes down to the table outside, overlooking the hills, and he arrived, announcing, "I've put on cologne. Now I won't smell so much."

When he had called earlier that morning, he had immediately told me that he might come by in the afternoon for a quick visit but that he couldn't come to lunch because his hosts were preparing lunch for him—did I know them? I said no, and that it was too bad he couldn't come. He said, well, he had to speak to his hostess, he would call again, maybe he could come to lunch. It is always so with him. He never asks. He merely talks and as he does so, something in his timing, the slightest hesitation, if one is attuned to him, can lead one to deduce what he might at that moment have his heart lightly set on. If one says nothing, the moment will pass leaving no trace of a request having been either made or denied, just a rise in the temperature of words. It is the one communication, aside from all the French, Italian, Greek, Egyptian, Spanish, English, that the Sephardim know. Most people speak the silent voice of the subconscious—whether it is by the movement of their body or by the spaces between words as they utter them—but very few understand it. I don't want to glorify this skill—it is one that Sephardim share with certain hotel concierges, waiters, and diplomats in general: being able to see what sort of weather is coming over the people around them.

Pierre sent off letters to two different Italian Catholic missions in Uganda, the Fratelli Bianchi and another, which works with AIDS patients—30 percent of the population—to volunteer to spend six months there, "renewable for another six."

"My friend at the Gay Men's Health Crisis wanted me in New York," he said, "but they have more than enough people there, don't you think? I feel they need me more in Uganda." Then he added almost frivolously, "I'll spend winter in Africa," purposely mimicking the tone of one who wants to make it sound like the swank thing to do. "I'm not afraid to die, I'm old," he adds, "it would be quite all right for me to die now."

He had taken a bite out of an open sandwich and said, "I want another slice on top of this one, immediately." He discarded the skin of the salame in a bronze ashtray at his elbow. Bambù, the smiling blue-eyed dog, had swept by his knees and inhaled it. "Go away," Pierre said, waving one hand in a circular motion, "no dogs please, I don't like dogs and they always like me . . . same with babies, I don't like them either . . ."

We had lunch under the vines, overlooking the hills. He tasted the tagliatelle. "It's not the worst pasta I've ever tasted, not at all," he announced and one felt that he was witholding criticism, probably regarding the sauce, not quite spicy enough,

45

or a little too sweet because the tomatoes were very ripe. He didn't have a second helping. He had some salad, though, and zucchini, and peach ice cream, saying to my mother, "I never eat ice cream, but since you made it yourself . . ." He touched his belly. "It all goes here, thank God, very easy to lose in four days at home in Gargnano, but today we gained weight well."

"I'm shutting the door. Don't come in—I'll be naked," he said as I led him into the child's room, my old room, where he was to have his siesta.

It lasted barely ten minutes: "I slept a very deep sleep." We sat in the kitchen as he had his coffee, and talked about Alexandria, where I was about to go. "Well, so you'll meet Bernard de Zogheb . . . Your uncles *ne le fréquentaient pas . . .*," he said pleased once again to point out the social disparity between our families.

"But Aldo told me that he used to be very good friends with Bernard's brother, Charlie," I said mischievously.

"Oh, Charlie is another matter entirely," he said, disappointed, though later he divulged that it was he who had inherited most of the family fortune, "while Bernard, vague as he is, was not paying attention. Quite understandable too: Charlie has six children, Bernard would just spend it on himself, he doesn't need it anyway." Pierre always speaks as though he has an internal devil's advocate because no matter what he says, he instantly says something else that appears to refute any possible objection to what he has just stated—a Christian who intercedes to soften any criticism that might issue from his lips.

I told him that what was once our house, intact till ten years ago, was now half in ruin. Before a law was passed that stipulated that only a two-storey house could be built to replace an old two-storey house, in an attempt to stop speculators from secretly destroying Alexandria's landmark houses and building high-rises in their place, the current owners had pulled out all the windows and doors of the house in Bulkley, so it could collapse more easily. More than half of it was already reduced to a pile of rubble, columns, pediments, broken glass. "Which half?" my mother inquired, suddenly interested. I said, "Not the half with the arched glass façade and the two rocket bomb shells on either side"—the entrance from the garden. Pierre ran his hands over his belly again contentedly, "Still, we are here," he said "with our coffee, and wine, and *here*—we are very lucky, if you think what happened to millions of people."

"What else do I want?" he said after a pause. "Oh, onions, do you have red onions? Well then, I'd like four. Two is too little. Let's say, a minimum of four."

His previous host was a man who wrote a book about the Arab world. "Do you like him?" I asked. "*Ni*," he replied, an Italian word combining *sì* and *no*. "He is very opinionated," Pierre continued, "travels a lot, knows everyone, just saw Shevardnadze, told me a few things about him, but I agree with him: there is no hope for Islam, it will simply fall apart. The PLO is falling apart. Have you seen the newspapers today? They're getting rid of Arafat. Saddam is against Assad. It's all just about killing still. It will never come to anything, they won't manage it."

We walked to his car. A case of Chianti was propped up on the roof of it. "My grandmother Evelyne Filus and your great-grandmother Gabrielle Tilche were cousins, and she doesn't remember," Pierre said nodding in the direction of my mother, "but I was at her wedding . . . There were two pheasants with the head and the tail stuck back on, reconstituted on the buffet table. Pheasants had never been seen before in Egypt. I quickly ate some because I had never tasted pheasant."

He carried a shopping bag in which there were quite a few more than the four onions requested. He opened the door of the car; I took his hand and kissed it, complaining that there was no ring on it. "I have a right to one, you know," he set me straight, "and to a red moiré robe, and to the miter," the tall hat, "but not to the pastoral staff—that's only for bishops."

"Well, you are a monsignor," my mother chided him, "are you not?"

"Yes, a canonical monsignor, and a parish priest" he said, sighing. "I asked my bishop, I saw him just the other day, if I could retire and he said, no, come on, do it for another two or three years." He told one of our guests that he had been a parish priest for many years: "Cicciolina was one of my parishioners," he volunteered. He can always find someone to mention that the other person will at least have heard of.

"Well, you make a good parish priest, don't you?" I said.

Quietly, without false modesty, he nodded: "I do."

As he was driving off, he opened a crack for the next flutter of change in his plans, which was to spend two nights at his next destination: "If I return, you could let me sleep on one of the couches, no?"

"Pierre, if you get bored and decide to come back, you can have a lovely bed—the house is full of them."

"I won't be bored."

I drove down to Pierre's house in Gargnano for one day in the hope of gathering some information before my trip to Alexandria. We would take his car, he would drive, I would pay for half the gas. All of his unpriestly impatience, I realized, was concentrated in his driving. Like one at the wheel of a Maserati, he dogs slow-moving vehicles until he can overtake them, honks his horn if they don't move out of the way, and throughout the trip is infuriated by any crossing, truck, traffic light, that will delay him. We had the entire Sunday before us and yet he decided we should leave one hour earlier than we had at first agreed to. As soon as we arrived, and had parked the car below the lemon groves by his diminutive stone house filled with books and precious mementos from friends, most of them famous, he began to say that it looked as though the fog might descend after all, and it would be safer to leave at three rather than four. Four became three, which became two.

We kept our coats on, as the house hadn't been heated in over two weeks (he had been to Spain and Rome), and upstairs he showed me where he kept his books on Egypt. He had several copies of Zogheb's comic operettas set to the tune of pop songs: *Le Sorelle Brontë* contained the scene of "Emiglia" Bronte's death, set to "The Beer Barrel Polka" and "Fools Rush In," presided over by a priest, presumably Pierre, and was once performed in New York, thanks to James Merrill who had an admiration for Zogheb. Ever since he was in his teens, Bernard could perform an entire operetta, singing all the roles himself.

I discovered that Pierre had probably the only remaining copies of Bernard's comic operettas as Bernard had only one of each, his own. To give something to Pierre is to have it be punctiliously preserved, at least for as long as he is alive. He has the entire collection of one publisher's books and running his eyes over the neat rows, he said, "Number one hundred and fifty-two is missing. Remind me to ask for it." The recipient of his request, when I saw him two days later, groaned comically, "Did he say there was a number missing? There always is." But Pierre is Pierre and though people might complain of his demands, and only behind his back, he always gets what he wants because for some magical reason, people *want* him to. It must be that they believe in his direct, or indirect, power to save them, hence damn them, too, or shall we say, not save them— the precinct of a priest, if he were in any way vindictive, which he isn't; still, he inspires a degree of awe besides the more pressing compulsion to invite him to lunch, dinner, anything, anyplace, where he might encounter prospective members of his electronic parish.

For now that he no longer has a parish, he "takes on" whoever comes his way and shows an interest. Food attracts him; new people attract him. He can be peremptory in his requests to meet ever new and interesting people: *"Qui tu me présente?"* And if one thought one was going to have dinner with him alone, he calls two or three times before the appointed day, asking innocently, "How shall I dress? Can I wear my jeans or should I wear my collar? How many people will be there?" At which point one might scramble around for someone new to feed him: writers and artists please him best.

Now, on my way to Egypt, it was my turn to say to him, *"Qui tu me présente?"* And he was willing to help but like a princess in a mystical Persian tale: first I would have to overcome several dreadful obstacles, the very first being his own unwillingness to part with anything his, even if it weren't strictly his, such as a person's telephone number. He did however give me a few invaluable names of the last bearers of the Atmosphere in Alexandria and he waved a manuscript under my nose, a family saga, that promised to bare many a secret and many a commonplace detail of everyday life in Alex in the forties. But he had sworn to guard those secrets, and though he said that I could come and read the manuscript at his house, I could not take it with me to Milan, photocopy it, and return it to him the next day. So I did not even look at it, as I had long ago decided to give in to the grain of things and include only what came towards me eager to be included.

At a table in his kitchen, still wearing our coats, we ate one hundred grams of spaghetti each with olive oil, garlic, and chili.

Later, I sat up in Pierre's study and looked at autographed copies of books by writers who were close friends of his. I opened Tondelli's last book at random and found Pierre quoted as having said to him, "We must do all that is in our power, even though we know it to be absolutely useless." Half priest, half pragmatist, Pierre has expressed his views on religion in two books. In one entitled *The Lightness of the Cross*, he sees Buddhism as "love cauterized into compassion," and though he thinks that the Buddha is perhaps "the most extraordinary man that ever lived," he finds that Jesus of Nazareth has "something more."

Of Bernard, Pierre said, "Give him my love. He usually travels for three months every winter . . . tell him I've got his drawing hanging in my kitchen, that you saw it . . . He's very *potinier*, very sociable . . . very cultured in an odd Alexandrian way." Then he added slyly, *"Tu va rencontrer tous les gens que tu n'avais jamais fréquentés de ta vie"* (You will meet all the people you never frequented in your life). Never, when? I wondered. When I was three years old? "Mind you, they know your uncles. Your father, also. *Probable, mais pas sûr.*" He expressed his doubts as to whether I had the right pedigrees; he wavered between yes and no. My father's family, no. My mother's family, yes. But even so, my grandfather, not really, my grandmother, yes. What confused him, I think, is that he intimately knew and liked some of these "no's" in spite of himself. I believe it is what drove him out of Alexandria and the Atmosphere forever.

Pierre and I were born in the same city; we are of the same race and both Catholics, though he converted whereas I am one since birth; we can speak in several languages together and yet, though I know he likes me, he questions whether I am as good as he, genetically—and we are cousins, and he is a priest. Once an Alexandrian, always an Alexandrian—I left too soon to be one. The sense of being different, and of being superior, though by a fraction only: add the matter of territory and you have a bloody war. What need is there to witness the killing? Every ritual, religious service, baptism, initiation, in the sweetest of peace times, is a killing, by the saying of what a person is, and isn't, a refutation of what others are, and aren't—the point where violence begins.

Stone animals have survived the appearance and disappearance of entire families. At the house in Alexandria we had a green serpentine marble seal on a pedestal in the garden. Anyone who spent any degree of time at that house was portrayed with the seal—straddling it, patting it on the head, standing by it. It was always somewhere in the picture. In the springtime, the seal had a large round bush of white daisies growing right beside it, and its nose seemed to be sniffing them. The seal is still there, in what used to be the garden, next to what used to be our house.

When I returned to Alexandria ten years ago, I searched for the house at the address my mother had given me. I looked for the garden. There were only buildings. Walking around the streets, looking up by accident, I saw my grandfather's initials on top of a tall iron gate, "s.p." I looked in between the bars of the gate: a man was playing with his dog. I waved to him, explained that this had been my grandfather's house. He opened the gate and offered to show me around.

On entering the house, I noticed the fresh barrenness of the rooms: though most of what had been in them had been removed, some pieces of art déco furniture remained. Because they were "new," I suppose my grandmother did not consider them good enough to take back to Europe. I remembered the house as vast and mysterious because many parts of it were not accessible to me—the kitchens, my grandparents' bedroom, the servants' quarters, the pantry, the cellar, the attic. Now it was all there, like a patient on a doctor's visiting table who has suffered terrible adversities but is there nonetheless, with enough residual strength to recover. The custodian kept repeating, as we walked around, "I am so sorry, I am so terribly sorry, but you will see, it will be turned into a center for studies." No crimson bougainvilleas hanging over the front arch at the entrance, no gazebo, no arched trellis covered by loofah vines, only the seraphic seal.

My father tells the story of how the first time he walked into the nursery to meet me just after I was born, and every subsequent time, I hollered uncontrollably. I earned myself the nickname "Siren of Zamalek" (after a nearby factory siren that went off punctually, in the morning and in the evening, with a drawn-out deafening squeal). He thought to himself, I'll show her. "After that, I walked in, said hello to your brothers, and ignored you. You never again cried when I came into the room."

I am holding a book of fairy tales. On the back cover, a picture in a round frame of a happy teddy bear holding a book between his legs. Propped up on his knees, a book with a teddy bear on the cover, holding a book with a teddy bear on the cover, holding a book with a teddy bear on the cover . . . Where will this end? I thought to myself. Another book had a gloating red face on its cover above a roast chicken that managed to look happy *in its every limb*.

The room cool, the shades drawn, the white cotton sheet against my cheek and the enforced rest: impossible to sleep in the middle of the day. Whispers with the other prisoner of this hour away from the garden and its freedoms, Gianchi. "Are you sleeping?" was the code to begin: whispers became murmurs and murmurs shouts. The door creaked open. We looked up. A tall ghost in a white shroud stood at the entrance, took a few steps towards the center of the room. "If you do not sleep," it said in Arabic, "I will come tonight and take you away." We shivered. The shroud withdrew. We never told on the ghost as telling would have made its threat more real. Years later, we discovered that the ghost consisted of the cook, Dahab, with one of our nannies, Athiat, on his shoulders, and a white *burnus* thrown over them. I think they were lovers because they had terrible arguments and she called him a donkey and one time they fought all the way around the house, into the garden, up a little wall and onto the roof of a nearby house. I followed them and when I reached the roof I noticed that my right arm had a gash in it where I had cut it on the broken glass that was embedded on top of the wall to keep robbers away. "Curiosity killed the cat," my grandmother admonished. Another proverb involving cats carried almost the reverse meaning: "A cat may look at a king," and she used it when she was in the mood to stare one down.

Giampi was the eldest and did not suffer the indignity of being paired off as Gianchi and I were: we wore matching grey outfits; whatever he did, I did; we woke up, had our bath, our nap, our meals, all at the same time. If we were to be trotted out in the course of my grandmother's interminable canasta parties to greet the guests and eat one of the impalpable anchovy paste sandwiches, we were trotted out together, and dismissed together. We accepted this twinness as a fact of life and I took it as a great betrayal when we became separate, or rather, when Gianchi abandoned me for our elder brother who treated him as a lackey and a built-in admirer of his every gesture, except when he lost his temper, and he would clench his fists, stick his tongue in between his teeth and go around the house kicking anything in the way. But Gianchi only became the "little lion," as we called him, when the world disappointed him. Fights with Giampi were always a battle of words. He could unleash a torrent of them and much as I tried to say something as cutting or conclusive as he had, I lost. He should have been a lawyer, my father sometimes said, and he is one now of lost causes he sometimes wins.

When Gianchi caught typhoid fever, it seemed unfair to me that he had got it instead of me. Acquaintances filed in bearing gifts, whispering sweetly at his bedside. Doctors talked among themselves. Servants brought hot liquids, cold liquids, potions, broths, yogurts, at regular intervals. He did not even have the grace to look sick. Aunt Sarah, the aunt of the blue eyes, came very often. One day she brought a pile of coloring books. She plopped them and herself down on Gianchi's bed, then picked one at random from the top of the pile, tossed it down at me sitting on the floor, and said conspiratorially to him, "There, we'll give that to the little monster."

Once, Gianchi and I had a big fight over a painted sandpail. He lost his temper, threw it at me and missed. I threw it back and got him right on the forehead. He had to be taken to the hospital, given a tetanus shot, and sewn up. I was punished because the action that achieves damage is publicly blamed. Intentions can remain secret.

In Alexandria, I looked up Bernard de Zogheb. "He doesn't have a telephone so you'll have to call Lucette de Saab and leave a message with her," Pierre had said, "I don't have her number but you can find it in the telephone book." To find a number through information, in Egypt, one needs a person's first and last names but also their three middle names; otherwise the operators are instructed to not even try. The concierge at the San Giovanni in Alex found the number, finally, of another acquaintance of Pierre's, at a clinic, who gave me the number of Lucette, with whom I left a message.

Bernard is wiry, his face weatherbeaten like that of a sailor; he has grey hair, the mouth of one accustomed with his lower lip to welcome a cigarette, sailor-like, and hold it there even while talking; quick but sober, he is a loner in every cell, dressed in a worn but noble blazer. He described the jobs that had come his way: newspaper stringer in Paris, tourist guide on a Greek island, among others. In the Alexandria of the forties and fifties, he had improvised his "operas" as a teenager for the amusement of his parents' assembled guests. "Can you guess who that is?" he said pointing to a black and white portrait of a languid young man, resting on a bookshelf in his living room. "Orson Welles?" I volunteered. "No, though it looks a bit like him: it's Farouk on the day that he learned of his father's death. I saved it from the scrap heaps of the newspaper I worked for in Paris—the archives were being cleaned out." There is to be a show, soon, of Bernard's watercolors: "I decided to concentrate on Egypt and leave out the French landscapes—who is going to care about a scene in Provence?"

With Bernard I went to the Jewish cemetery in Alexandria in the hope of finding the graves of my grandparents, Haco and Rebecca—my father had asked me to bring them flowers. I use the pronoun "them" as though they could still be alive, or present, hovering over the grounds of the cemetery, yet so confined as to have to wait there for one or another of their progeny to appear. Instructions were given to me by my father of how to find the graves: the old cemetery, not the new, the first cemetery, not the second. In Italy it had sounded so clear. In Alexandria, face to face with the last representatives of Alexandrian society, it was clear that nothing would be clear. The Western world of the practical codified for even the most philistine of outsiders had not touched Alexandria. Lucette thought no one had been buried in the old cemetery in the last hundred years. I gratefully accepted Bernard's offer to accompany me.

We walked to the cemetery from his house, and knocked on the iron gate. A guardian came. We intruded on an atmosphere of life—mongrels chasing each other, two children playing on the ground with little plastic buckets—that gave an air of obsolescence to the graveyard, as though the souls confined to that earth had been exiled to be among living beings who knew nothing of them. The guardian, a man in his forties, asked who we were looking for, and when I told him the names, pretended to know, and led us here and there, till it became apparent that our own instincts might prove a better guide, if only for the pleasure of following our own wrong leads.

I remember it as a comical occasion: Bernard tripping along the narrow paths between marble slabs sometimes cracked by a growth of weeds, now and then stooping to read an inscription or call out a name to me. There were many names he recognized. We looked among the huddle of neoclassical pavilions that the more prominent families had built. The Tilches, my maternal grandmother's family, had one of these, but we didn't go in, I suppose because we had little time, and I was eager to fulfill my father's errand.

I saw only one family grave—that of my great-uncle Ezio Pinto, my grandfather's brother. It was a distinguished one: a slab of white marble with the name inscribed in block capitals, and his dates; to the side, set on a diagonal, an unadorned marble bench, and behind it a freestanding arch that enclosed the air, the earth, the sky around the grave, into an open-air parlor for the visitor.

Twenty years after a death, even those who witnessed the burial, visited the grave many times bringing flowers, cannot muster the precision to explain to an outsider how to reach the site; and so the site is forgotten. What I saw was a great deal of marble, a derelict graveyard made gay by its dereliction, for only a graveyard well maintained is a true place of mourning.

We walked to the Elite restaurant. Its owner of half a century, Madame Cristina, has six original manuscripts of Cavafy's poems which she sent to her son in Athens, along with other cherished possessions that she lives in constant dread of being dispossessed of, having seen it happen to countless friends in the past, though not recently: "*On sait jamais,*" she said gently.

The Egyptian waiter brought the first in a long series of *mezé*—taramosalata, stuffed grape leaves—and beers for Bernard and myself. Madame Cristina said the help was not what it used to be: "*Ce n'est pas comme avant . . . c'est fini ici pour les Européens.* If you ask them to polish the glass door, they say, 'Tomorrow.' Before they would say, 'Yes, Madame,' and bow, and be grateful that you had taught them how to do it."

She walks one hundred and forty-three steps up to her apartment because there is no elevator, although she is well into her seventies. At night, after closing the restaurant, she confesses, it's tiring. She says she likes to have her first Turkish coffee of the day in bed so when her maid comes, she goes to open the door for her, then runs back to bed and the woman knows to bring her coffee. Every day, she arrives at the Elite at nine in the morning and stays until one the next morning. She takes her place at the cash register by the entrance, concealed from the waist down by a door that serves as a counter: she appears to have been built into her sentinel post. She sits wrapped in a large black and white shawl—her long face, blond-tinted hair, flinty eyes made smaller and intensified by the lenses of her glasses—perched over the flowers, supervising the movements, conversation, humor of her patrons.

The walls of the restaurant are covered with old posters announcing exhibitions of Matisse and Braque, Rio de Janeiro at carnival time, and a Picasso-like blue and white painting of two bulls. The kitchen for salads is below, the big kitchen is up one flight. Beyond the immediate walled restaurant is what she calls *la véranda*, a sidewalk café she eventually had enclosed in a navy and white arklike wooden structure in which there are red banquettes much like the ones to be found in New York's Greek coffee shops.

Some salty fried cheese balls arrived, and little meatballs in tomato sauce, squid, a salad of *garghyr* (watercress), cucumbers and tomatoes, and tahini ("*Mafish kalamata,*" the waiter told her: no more olives), and a dish of lemons cut in half, the Egyptian kind, which are round, yellow, much smaller than limes, and sweeter.

From the items on the menu that Madame Cristina described with anachronistic flourish—" . . . *le poulet negresco, c'est un plat somptueux*"—Bernard ordered a *côtelette de veau pané* (breaded veal cutlet) which came with zucchini and matchstick fries, and I had fried squid. I was startled to find when it arrived that it consisted of three very large pieces of squid fried whole. Having come to sit with us, Madame Cristina ordered a doll's ration: a hamburger the size of a communion wafer, and six or seven matchstick fries on a small plate.

The conversation was strangely torpid, as though sub-merged—anything said took time to travel from one person to another. I knew neither of them very well, and they knew each other too well: we were either past or before the point of intimate conversation. Three sibylline Alexandrians—a rarity. With Bernard there is a strange reserve. He is amicable but *closed*, like his watercolors of Provençal landscapes, which seem to willfully ignore the last century of transformations—representations of that famous time, *avant*, which to an Alexandrian can mean anything from before modern times to before Nasser, and before "losing everything"; the expression is *"ils ont tout perdu."*

Madame Cristina asked whether I liked Yves Montand, and had the man who replaced her at the cash register play "Les Feuilles Mortes," then Juliette Gréco singing the same song. Montand had come to her restaurant. He had told her that she had a Greek profile. She asked me to confirm this, turning sideways and saying, with a hint of coquettishness, "Do I have a Greek profile?" I reassured her.

At first the restaurant had been managed by her Greek husband and, imitating herself cowering, Madame Cristina showed me how she had slunk about in the shadows meekly, while he delivered orders. "He sued me sixty times," she said, "and lost every time, till he was banned from entering the street." He went to work as a waiter in another restaurant, and has since died. Now she feels she can soar, she said, free as a bird, and she lifted and dropped her elbows rhythmically, as though they were wings.

There was a Doctor Yasoulis, a Jew, she said, who had refused to leave Alexandria at the time when most Jews, and foreigners in general, had left, some of them at twenty-four-hour notice, abandoning most if not all their possessions, and being forced to sell their houses for a pittance. This Yasoulis, a cellist, sold all his belongings one by one in order to survive, and finally was obliged to sell his cello with which he had given concerts around town and made a modest living. Still, he considered Alexandria his city. He would come to the Elite and Madame Cristina would feed him. The Egyptian police remonstrated with her: why was she helping him? He needed to eat, she gave him food, was that so bad? But why, they insisted, did she have to choose a Jew? She didn't choose a Jew, she said, and showed them how she also fed impoverished Greeks. Yasoulis ended up in an old people's home and died soon after.

"Your uncle Boaz," said Madame Cristina, "was such a good-looking man, so cultivated and interested in art and literature. He would come here by himself and he would sit there." She indicated the back of the restaurant. "He ordered *escalope de veau* and many little salads. Then after he finished his lunch, I would send him a pack of Gauloises, he would light one up, and he was happy. He was a flirt and if there was a beautiful woman, he would say to me, 'She is lovely, no?' "

Boaz ended up marrying Cristina's daughter, who was faithful to him through the harder years of his life in Rome where he had set up a clothing emporium, till his sudden death, days before turning sixty. Cristina traveled to Rome for the funeral. She arrived after it was over, having waited all night at the airport in Cairo for her plane to leave. She was so distraught with worry and grief that she did not recognize her own son when he came to open the door for her. I think Madame Cristina was herself a little in love with my uncle Boaz, his straight thick eyebrows, sharp green eyes under heavy lashes, straight nose, sculpted mouth, and like many mothers before her introduced him to her daughter so he might remain near. It is said that he was a spy for the Mossad. My only memory of him: he gave me a book by Benjamin Disraeli.

Madame Cristina has been at the Elite since 1952, a year after my birth. At any moment, she thinks that she might be forced to leave. But she seems prepared.

I walked around the *quartier grec*, where most of the rarefied Jewish families had lived, those of the Atmosphere—art nouveau houses, quiet ordered streets, trees. Later, at the San Giovanni, in my "suite," consisting of two lopsided little rooms, with a terrace larger than either overlooking Stanley Bay, I transcribed my notes, taken in Gargnano, of Pierre's memories of Alexandria:

"I couldn't stand the society though I loved the luxury. I was eleven when my parents divorced. I was born *à la maison*. It was an odd society—corrupt. Egypt between the wars was like Europe before World War I—still Edwardian, or Poincaré France. Everyone went to Europe in the summer, and sent their cooks to the Cordon Bleu in Paris. I've never eaten so well. The rugs, the china . . . the old Madame Salvago always washed her Louis XV Sèvres—all 283 pieces—with her own two hands after dinner parties.

"There were a lot of very pretty women in Alexandria. They had so much time to look after themselves. Now if you go to Alexandria . . . Lucette's birthday is two days before mine, she gave a party for me . . . there are people there whose name we wouldn't even have known once. It was so snobbish, it was incredible. And we were very cultivated. We'd read Sartre,

Proust. We knew all of English literature. I had read everything by the time I was eighteen. I was five when Cavafy died. He was *employé à la* Société des Eaux of which my grandfather was a stockholder . . . My grandfather had a fondness for Cavafy. He took me to see him at the Hôpital Grec, just before he died, and Cavafy caressed my hair. One of my grandfather's classmates at a German elementary school was Rudolph Hess. I remember how excited he was when Hess landed in Scotland. Hess's father was a cotton broker.

"We are well-born on both sides. My great-grandfather was Grand Rabbin of Constantinople. Your grandparents' marriage, Tilche and Pinto, was a *mésalliance* . . . The Pintos were at the periphery of Alexandrian society. The Alhadeffs even more. The Pintos were in it a bit because of your grandmother Berthe and your great-grandmother Gabrielle who were Tilche. It was a very closed group . . . for the Jews, the Rolos, the Menasces, the Cattaouis; for the Greeks, the Salvagos, the Zervudakis, the Benakis, the Choremis; for the Syrians, the de Saabs, Michalla Pasha; for the Copts, the Khayats. Winnie was first cousin to Boutros Boutros-Ghali. I am going to see Lea Boutros-Ghali tomorrow afternoon. Chez la vieille Madame Salvago, the exiled kings of Greece lived there. *La société* was very very closed and very snobbish. I'm sure they were very promiscuous . . .

"Joyce Ades, who later became Breton's girlfriend, was the first person I ever loved—I was very much in love with her when I was sixteen. She wrote me letters from the King David in Jerusalem—she refused to send me her pornographic poems, though. She died of cancer like her mother, her father, her brothers.

"I left when I was eighteen to go to Cambridge, immediately

after the war. I had an M.A. at twenty-one 'cause I'm clever. I did no work at all. I discovered that literature was no use: I had to study philosophy. I was very naïve. Wittgenstein taught me the limits of reason. I'm very grateful to him for that. I was Wittgenstein's last student: twice I had him. With an honors degree you get an M.A. automatically. I got a doctorate in theology in Rome. I was offered a job in Cambridge as a reader. I refused for one reason only—the weather.

"I was twenty-four. I converted. In Cambridge I had shelved the problem. In the last scene of Bernard's operetta, *Le Sorelle Brontë*, there's a priest—introduced when I went back to Egypt as a priest. My grandmother—Evelyne Aghion, another very good family—was very upset. She was already upset I had become a Catholic. The night after my arrival there was a big party and I was horrified I wasn't invited. I told my best friend Jackie Rolo, 'Apparently I am not wanted.' Her mother Yvonne was a *grande dame* . . . They had a lovely house in Alex with a *service impeccable* (mind you, you had that often at your grandmother Berthe's). Now it's the German Cultural Institute. All of the royalty in exile came to that house. Yvonne's husband, Max, was president of the Sporting Club and his brother, Robert, was president of the Jewish Community. Béjart was giving a performance at the Cinéma Mohammed Ali. The next day I had a phone call from Yvonne, inviting me. She had a central loge. 'Pierre, dear,' she told me, 'why don't you come and sit right in front?' It was all Yvonne's doing if Egyptian society accepted me after my conversion.

"When Jackie became a Catholic, everyone blamed me. I wrote to Yvonne: 'I'm sorry if it upset you, but it had nothing to do with me.' Everyone in Egypt thought we'd get married.

Yvonne replied, 'You know how Jewish I am, but if it makes Jackie happy . . .' She was a superior for seven years at the Grail Community near London.

"*En Alexandrie, personne ne réfléchissait*, people didn't think, and suddenly, like a stone thrown into a hothouse, someone they knew well had made choices. Jean de Menasce, whose father was also president of the Jewish community, became a Dominican. He was Larry Durrell's uncle-in-law, *iranisant*. He baptized my mother, gave her First Communion and married her, all in the same day, to Albert Camus—another Albert Camus, not the writer—in Paris . . . very nice.

"Claude Vincendon, whose mother Claire was Jean de Menasce's sister, married Lawrence Durrell. My first meeting with Durrell . . . I was eleven and I was asleep. My mother was giving a party. You know those electrical massage belts women used for slimming? I woke up and heard someone say, 'This is better than sex.' There was Durrell, standing completely naked in the bathroom with the belt around his backside, jiggling like a pudding."

Aunt Sarah, too, had lived in the *quartier grec*, in a vanilla-colored apartment building with round windows like those of a ship:

"I knew Pierre when he was sixteen or seventeen. He took the streetcar to go to Victoria College every day and knitted scarves along the way. On Friday evening, he would go to the Jewish quarter and distribute them to the poor. He already had the soul of a priest.

"Then suddenly, he converted. I don't take him seriously. It's not true, for instance, when he says that people in Egypt sent their cooks to be trained at the Cordon Bleu. The Rolos had superb houses. King Farouk used to go and play cards with them. He could never stand to lose, so he would stay until three or four in the morning, until he won. I was living on the rue des Pharaons and I used to see Robert Rolo often, *il était charmant*. They were *type anglais*, one saw that in Egypt—all that surrounded them was very fine, the furniture, the people. Snobbism was the number one quality in Egypt. It was the *crétins* who were snobs . . . that too was because people had time. Some people pretended to be English but they were born in Egypt. They always seemed constipated.

"I am just talking, but you will do an *épuration* of the text.

"When I think about it now, it was a life of *cocottes* that we led: one took care of the house a little bit, one did the more pleasant things that needed to be done. The rhythm was slow, as in all countries that have a warm climate. We went to have coffee on the rue Shérif. Then we went shopping at Hannaux—*très chic, très grand*. It was on two floors and sold everything: handbags, shoes, dressing gowns, *petites robes d'été*, men's things, too. But for an elegant dress we went to the seamstress. We had a great deal of time. We went to Le Salon Vert for fabrics. With my mother we had to go to every single store and get many samples from each. Then, at home, we had to remember where each sample came from.

"The seamstress—usually Greek—would bring over some patterns from Paris, and slips in natural silk. My hairdresser was Greek, too. Everyone had hair-sets done with *bigoudis*, or they had their hair frizzed so they could look like little sheep. I kept my hair long-long, and black-black. When it started to go white, I cut it.

"I would go and pick up my father at eleven every day and

we would go to the Sporting Club, or to the Yacht Club. People played bridge. There was a swimming pool and many tennis courts. My mother never came. Shopping for food? The cook usually took care of that. I ordered the meat and the vegetables. I went to the market sometimes for the fruit, the coffee, the cheese. It was not so easy, a different shop for each thing, but we had time.

"La Scala came to Alexandria and La Comédie-Française, wonderful concerts, film premières where people got all dressed up. The Egyptian high-society ladies were all Turkish. King Farouk was white—Ottoman. All the princesses were beautiful. The women in Alex were excessively beautiful.

"The Swiss only saw one another, but the Greeks, the Italians, the French, the Jews, when there were parties they were all there together. There was no anti-Semitism then. There was no sectarianism.

"There were many dinners in Alex, with many guests and lovely tables. People asked me in America whether there were crocodiles in Cairo and I was tempted to leave them in their ignorance, but I couldn't, I told them, 'No, there are no crocodiles in Cairo, that's higher up the Nile.' People imagine that Egypt was a savage country . . .

"There was a lot of time, a lot of intrigue. Everything was known—it was a little place. You saw, you knew, though certain things were not discussed. Often it was not out of love but out of interest that women had affairs. It was a society where to be well dressed and to be invited to dinners and theaters was important and some didn't have the means for it. So they had affairs. Jewels were important, and furs, in spite of the mild climate. I think you have to have time to make mischief. We had servants . . .

"In Egypt, servants were martyrized. The wife of one of the best eye doctors in Alexandria used to beat her servants with a slipper. Whites treated blacks like slaves. In the thirty-three years I lived in Egypt, I had four servants, of whom two stayed with me till the very end. The Sudanese were wonderful . . . I had a cook and a *sufraghi*. In general, the Sudanese were very honest and very *stylé* also. They knew how to dress well and how to set the table. When they served at the table they wore a turban, a striped or white silk galabiya. They had a room in our building. They left their wives in the Sudan and they would go and visit them when we left in the summer. Abdul I hired when he was seventeen. The day I left Egypt for good, he came to see me off at the harbor. He wrapped himself around a light pole and that's the way I remember him as the boat pulled out.

"We left the house with everything in it, even the carpets. I knew a man who bought permits for Greeks, who were persona grata, to take their belongings out of the country. He would re-sell the permits to us. The shipment would go to Athens, where the address would be changed to an address we had given in Italy. Sometimes the things were stolen first, and never arrived at their destination.

"I felt I had roots in Alexandria. After I left, I never felt that ever again. My whole family was there. Now I have to go round and round—Italy, Belgium, America—to see them all and I'm half dead with fatigue. I can't do this much longer . . ."

III

An island within an island, within an island: on the island of Rhodes, the island of Sephardic Jews and within it, the island of one family—my father's. To separate, and separate again, as though to eliminate difference altogether; but Aunt Rachel, my grandmother's sister and oldest living member of that family, now at the end of her long life, ensconced in a one-bedroom apartment of a hotel on the island of Manhattan, if she encounters Sephardic Jews from Rhodes who were carpet haulers she knew as a young woman she does not acknowledge them: "They are not of my rank," she says, "if she imagines that just because she is wearing a mink coat, I will talk to her, she is wrong." This rank is one she believes God himself has entitled her to. Stooped, ninety-five, an ancient bird that has outlived its destiny but continues to guard its plumage, she has just enough vision left to scrutinize the surrounding air for ghosts but none for oncoming traffic. "They can't run us over, we are *judíos*," she says gravely. The rank must be upheld: if she goes to the doctor, she wears her black lace boned corset, little heels, a thin belt to emphasize her waist. And first she will go to the hairdresser and powder her beak, though all of her body has gathered at the center axis as though ready to be lifted up to the heavens—a stele preparing to stand over a tomb, mourn her own passing. Life protracts itself like a white leader at the end of a film for her and she fills it with every liberty senility allows her brain to take.

She has already died, properly speaking, twice: once when her husband died but that was a life he had brought her into. They had married late: for seven years he tarried; she, meanwhile, received the advances of an *imbécile* who left her little notes, tickets to the cinema. But it was Sammy she wanted: *"Yo lo quiero, yo lo tengo que tomar,"* she said. Then, at last, a telegram arrived from her family in Izmir saying, "Sammy has decided to marry you, come quickly, we are waiting for you"— not exactly a proposal. The same day a large basket of flowers was delivered to her; she thought they were from Sammy, but they were from the *imbécile*.

She died again when her son died suddenly of a stomach ailment. She had drawn him back into her womb, little by little, seven phone calls a day to his office, breathing his air even through the telephone wire. He can't have known what it was like to be born, to be outside the womb, the cord cut. Even now, they are indissoluble. "I go shopping," she sobs, "and when I come home, there is someone, always there is someone, and it's him. He speaks to me, 'Why do you carry heavy parcels?,' he asks. He is there all night, I make myself sick, all night, I take a Valium."

She died when he died but she returned, cast the cord once again, like an able fisherwoman, into her telephone receiver and hooked my uncle, the gynecologist living in Queens, her nephew. She calls him seven or eight times a day for twenty minutes, an hour, hangs up, forgets she has just spoken to him, calls again. He is thinking of moving to another continent.

When he arrived in America with his Italian medical degree, and several kilos heavier than the forty he had weighed when he had left Auschwitz, she took him under her wing. Blue-eyed, awkward, timid he must have been. Aunt Rachel introduced him to his future wife, on a Sabbath at the synagogue. Still, he didn't know then that he would have to thank her with every breath almost fifty years later.

In the basement of his neo-Tudor house, women shuttle back and forth between the little examining rooms with their stirruped reclining armchairs, and the doctor's office, where the talking is done and the eyes never fail to rest on the plastic replica of a uterus, complete with ovaries and fallopian tubes—a cannibal's see-through lunchbox.

"It's hot, it's damp, it's dark in there," Nissim ruminated, "if you have two germs, they become two million."

"One should put a lightbulb," his sister Sarah suggested gravely.

". . . fertile ground, perfect for infections. They wear nylons, pants, then they call me, 'Doctor, I am dying, I have to see you tonight,'" Nissim continued.

"A lightbulb and some ice, too," Sarah finished her thought.

"A gynecologist shouldn't speak like that," his wife scolded.

"Shouldn't spit in the dish he eats from," said the gynecologist.

A woman had better not be jealous if she marries a dedicated midwife of a man. All through their years of marriage, whenever he left for a delivery, in the middle of the night, or at dawn, Ketty would lean out the upstairs window and wave goodbye to him as he got into the car. His patients, the Greek ones especially, brought him pastries, bread puddings, *caciocavallo* cheese—sometimes instead of a fee. He gave up doing

72

deliveries since the cost of his insurance was almost as high as his revenue, but the cost of this deprivation cannot be calculated. He has sought refuge among his investments, applying himself to getting numbers to conceive and multiply. He has kept his wife in the office near him for decades—that old-fashioned thing: sacrifice. The extreme fragility of two people whose organisms are intertwined: she does his will, for the bulk of their life, and he does hers when they travel further and further away from home.

He gave up being at the beck and call of hundreds of women only to be at the beck and call of a single imperious one—Aunt Rachel. She discussed all of her bodily functions, a privilege even her son must have been spared. He, a doctor, lent his ear to all her intimacies, from the rumbling of her grief to that of her gall. And the persecutions began: she saw thieves and murderers everywhere and they were her rivals in the affections of her son, first, then of her nephew. She, the self-immolating effigy of "what we once were," of that famous rank, accused one family member of stealing a brooch, another of murdering her son, *"Lo mató, lo mató,"* she wailed. *"Oui, chérie,"* the doctor soothed absentmindedly, and his wife, in the background, muttered exasperated, "He should say, '*Non, chérie.*' If she speaks like that in front of strangers, they'll think she's crazy and take her straight to an insane asylum."

Rachel and Rebecca—the two sisters from Izmir with twenty years between them. Rachel's favorite game was to pretend to be French and to speak a language she had invented to make herself out to be more sophisticated than she was: it was a combination of Ladino and the three words of English she knew.

Their house in Izmir was in a quarter called Carataj. "Say it was in Juseraki, *hanoum*, it's more chic," Aunt Rachel instructed, "Carataj is like Brooklyn." The house had a garden and at the end of it, the sea, cabins on stilts shrouded by curtains, behind which the women, covered from head to toe, sat submerged to their neck for hours, chattering, as the children swam.

Rachel and Rebecca's only brother became a jeweler: an ornate silver filigree basket we had at home that had been warped into wobbliness over the years was something he had made. Their father Shalom had been a jeweler, too. He was tall and straight, had light eyes, a mighty beard and wore a red tarbush as all Turks did, with a black pompon swinging from it. He spent the last years of his life in Constantinople and spoke Hebrew, which led my father to suppose he was a rabbi, as hardly anyone else in the family spoke it. He was a delicate man obsessed with hygiene: when he embraced his children, later his grandchildren, he would lean forward, peck their cheek, then kiss his own fingers. Rebecca inherited that squeamishness—she never drank from anyone else's glass, and her comment of love when her husband died was that never in all the years she had been married to him had she found his underpants soiled when he took them off at night.

My father gave me a black and white photograph of his mother, and one of his father, side by side under a slab of plexiglass. Grandfather Haco has a v-shaped hairline. Three things stand out in his face: thick eyebrows uninterrupted across the bridge of the nose, shaded coal-black eyes; a moustache thick and wide beneath the nostrils like a poisonous exhalation, then suddenly lifted up at either end into whimsical curled wisps

74

that make light of the gravity of the rest of the face; a diminutive bow tie affixed to a very high, starched collar—brows, moustache, tie—a man of solid worth tied in bows and presented to my grandmother Rebecca.

Hers is a round face (later, it became gaunt, and the cheekbones emerged)—light eyes poised between surprise and illumination, reflecting minerals fallen into the quiet folds of a face. She wears a light-colored wide-brimmed hat set at an angle on her dark curls and surmounted by a vaporous ostrich feather, erupting, then vanishing into misty photographic emulsion. Small mouth, shapely budding lips, resolute chin. The white lace trim of the black dress becomes a curled petal at the back of her neck, offering a tender ledge from which to view the formidable will. She could be his mother.

As a boy working for his elder brothers in the family firm he was given an allowance which he set aside till he had enough to start his own banking and trading firm. The brothers and cousins became competitors as the island of the family split into two. The older family firm dropped its interest rates; my grandfather raised them and customers flocked, believing the higher rates to be a sign of health. Haco prospered.

The name Alhadeff is Arabic: *Al* means "the," and *hadeff*, or *khadiv*, means "señor." In Turkey we were told it stands for "the javelin thrower" and somewhere else, for "the one who aims straight." I have spent hours, a minute here, a minute there, spelling it on the telephone in every country in the world. In our pronunciation, the *h* has become silent. In Arabic that is incorrect—so we mispronounce our name, while others misspell it: Abladeff, Adaleff, Alphabet . . .

There was an Alhade in the 1400s, who was born in Sicily, and lived first in Syracuse, then Palermo, author of a book titled *Discurso del Oro*, published in Venice, on the weights and measures mentioned in the Bible. He was an astronomer, who wrote liturgical and satirical poems, and died at the age of thirty-three.

When did the family first reach Spain? And then, was it Córdoba or Andalusia? We know only that they must have left following the Decree of Catholic Laws, refusing to convert so that my father could do so, canceling out in one stroke a millennium of dogged devotion. Still, he is a Sephardic Jew who married another Sephardic Jew, and though he has now undone that marriage, we, his children are purebred Sephardic Jews, the last of our breed, who have not married Sephardic Jews, when we have married. I find this fact wonderful and perplexing: centuries of keeping the race "pure," then suddenly, the discipline gone, the genes contaminated, the free-for-all. Was all the separateness, the loyalty to one religion, the undilutedness, worth it? We are just remnants of a reason for a strange unwarranted pride, on one side, for violence, on the other. Remnants. We may as well have been plain mortals all along, gotten a head start on the present filled with mixed mortals whose list of origins will grow, be multiplied by four, eight, sixteen, till listing them all will have become the sole precinct of esoteric databases, and the final compounds might resemble each other in fundamental nature like teas and tobaccos— a different fragrance here, note of amber there, but still tea and tobacco.

Sultan Mehmet II wanted Jews with their chameleon abilities for commerce, banking, languages, trading. Between 1492 and 1522, date of the conquest of Rhodes by Soliman the Mag-

nificent, the Alhadeffs landed in some port of Anatolia, perhaps Izmir. Somehow, they later reached Rhodes. Soliman was
eager to counterbalance the influence of Christian Greeks on
the economy.

The first remembered ancestor, Hadji Behor, known as
H.B., was born in Rhodes in 1783 and died in Jerusalem in
1880. His own father died in Bodrum, across from the island
of Cos, and had to be shipped to Rhodes for burial, which is
perhaps a sign that there was wealth in the family even then.
Unlike most Sephardic, or Spanish, Jews, H.B. was tall, blond
and had blue eyes. Like them, he wore a beard and a long black
caftan. His wife Esther was dark and minute. They had a son
called Jacobo, later known as Papu Yaco.

H.B. traded in cumin, pepper, cinnamon, tartaric acid, all
spices, but also in tobacco and hardware. He set up shop in a
disused mosque, now a Greek café, that remained the head
branch of the company he founded for one hundred and fifty
years.

A French traveler to Rhodes wrote of his encounter with a
"rich Jewish merchant" in 1843:

"We accepted with pleasure the French Consul's offer to
visit the Jewish quarter. After making our way through the
graveyard, we entered the city. A lame boy was sent ahead to
announce our arrival and he reappeared with a bearded old
man in tow. The Jew was enveloped in a sumptuous fur and
wore a black turban. His sons walked behind him. He advanced towards the captain of the frigate and bowed, bringing
his hand to his heart and to his lips. He bid us follow him
through various streets which were unlike those of the center

of Rhodes in that a profusion of flowers adorned windows and terraces, giving them a festive air.

"At the gates of his dwelling, the master waved away a crowd that had gathered, allowing only the family to enter. They removed their slippers and we found ourselves in a handsome hall supported by ancient columns. By the screened windows was a long sculpted platform covered with a Persian rug and silk mattresses. The merchant opened an ebony armoire containing rare Hebrew manuscripts. Simultaneously, the old man's sons opened a cedarwood chest and retrieved rolls of gold-embroidered linen, silk scarves in dazzling colors from which emanated the scent of jasmine and roses. After we had admired the fabrics, the merchant led us to a gallery overlooking the garden; a thick trellis stretched beneath the beams was weighed down with dewy foliage and hanging grapes. The master bid the captain sit on a settee while the little children giggled as they showed us how to sit on the square red silk cushions.

"Suddenly, the door flew open and three young girls appeared. One carried a basket of fruit on a bed of leaves, another pastries on white linen, and the third, a chiseled silver tray with jams, liqueurs, and glasses of water. They approached, shyly greeted us, and offered us refreshments. The eldest of these charming creatures was hardly twenty. They wore tight-fitting silk dresses shot with gold thread and laced up in front."

The description is of H.B., who was then fifty-one years old, of his house, the garden, known as *huerta chica*, and his children. The visit did not alter the French traveler's opinion of Jews. He concluded serenely: ". . . these pariahs of the East are reduced to an abject state. Never will you see on those faces dull as old coins the blush of shame: calumny and violence

78

pass, leaving no trace. The Jew hides his head beneath his upraised arm and like a dog comes to lie at the feet of his master . . . " The dog should have bit the Frenchman. I have seen
in my own family indiscriminate courtesy extended to
strangers. My mother fought the practice throughout her life
with my father.

The other side of the coin of courtesy is commerce. A Turkish
woman entered H.B.'s tent to buy a dozen handkerchiefs. She
asked Hadji Behor why such small handkerchiefs cost so
much. He answered: "*Hanoum*, the handkerchiefs seem small
only because the tent is so large." Another time, a peasant
complained to him about the price of a simple packet of pins
and he replied, "If you can make even one pin for this price, I
will give you the entire packet as a gift."

H.B.'s son, Papu Yaco, who was not a natural merchant, almost sold his share of the business to a Turk, Bekir Efendi, till
his brother Moreno threatened to hang himself and he was
obliged to give up the idea.

There was a great fire in Rhodes and Papu Yaco was almost
ruined. Men were hired to carry buckets of water and empty
them onto the iron door behind which the company's stores of
merchandise were kept. It is here that my grandfather Haco
makes his first remembered appearance: as a seven-month fetus in his mother's belly during her valiant efforts to save as
many rolls of fabric from the flames as she could.

H.B., who had gone to die in Jerusalem with his wife, returned when news of the fire reached him, "on an unsafe, filthy
ship," traveling "on deck," we are told. Why did he travel on
deck, when he was far from destitute? My own father, on a trip

79

to Bologna, to show his withered leg to the most illustrious orthopedic surgeon in Italy, was not allowed by his father to give his shirt to be washed or to buy another, as it was considered an extravagance. My father held his thumbs out so the dirty cuffs would not show. "Why do you hold your thumbs out?" his father tormented him. One should not mind expenses in the matter of health, but in the matter of appearances, pinch every penny.

After the long journey from Israel, H.B. got off the boat, walked directly to his store, caressed its walls, blessed the heavens, and said, "Now I can die in peace." Which he did a few years later: H.B. and his wife are both buried on the Olive Mount in Jerusalem.

Papu Yaco was my great-grandfather. His youngest born, Haco, a diminutive of Isaac, was my grandfather; the eldest was Salomon. There were some thirty years between the two brothers, which made it possible for Salomon's son Joseph to be much older than his uncle Haco.

Salomon's idea was simple and it made him rich: Turkey imported goods manufactured in Europe, and raw materials from Anatolia were exported to Europe. He exported sesame to the Balkans, carob to pharmaceutical plants, and acorns to tanneries in Europe; wood to Egypt for the construction of the railroad; styrax, a fixative for fragrances, to French perfumers. He traveled ceaselessly, and the list of his clients grew. He set the names of new manufacturers to music so as to remember them, and sang them on the train in a beautiful tenor voice as he traveled from place to place. He bought a house in a Turkish village called Kandilli. There he lived in isolation, and went about on a white mule from which he dismounted every time he encountered a Turkish dignitary. In town, within the walled city, he built a windmill in the midst of the orange and tangerine trees of the *huerta chica* to pump water into a pond for goldfish and frogs. On a windless day, as he sat astride one of its blades to remove the sail, he was lifted up high by a sudden gust, then dashed to the ground. But he was unhurt, so one grandson was named Nissim, which means "miracle," later nicknamed Nick. Nick was, by all accounts, "ugly as sin." He never married but was famous in Athens for his many women. He had diabetes, lost his sight and demanded a great deal of attention. His cook, the last of his lovers, took care of him. When he died, at the age of ninety-two, she spirited the corpse away, and his money, which she felt entitled to. There was no will.

Salomon, too, had diabetes, and every night drank great quantities of orange juice to quench his thirst, not knowing that it would precipitate his condition. He died in Vienna, where he had gone to consult a physician, on a bench at the railway station in 1909.

Salomon's son, Joseph, went to work for his father at the age of ten, taking down letters his father dictated to him in Spanish, translating them into French as he went along. He had a passion for Napoleon, could describe all his battles in detail, particularly the battle of Austerlitz. He told the anecdote of Napoleon looking out onto the plain at the Austrian army and declaiming, "*Cette armée est à moi!*" Metamorphosing into Napoleon himself, he would shout like one who must be heard across a limitless plain, "That army is mine!" Out of respect to the memory of his hero, Joseph's brother Ascher refused to stay at the Hotel Waterloo in London. Ascher was the cultivated one and Joseph the canny. Ascher seduced the gardener's wife and Joseph convinced the gardener, who had surprised them together, that he had imagined the entire episode.

In Rhodes, the Greeks were enemies of the Turks. The Jews were friends of both Greeks and Turks. The Greeks, who constituted the majority of the population and so a threat, were forced to leave the city at sunset when the cannon sounded, signaling the closing of the gates to the walled city. The Jews had their own quarter, the *judería*, near the Turks.

There were no schools except for the Talmud Torah until European consulates were established. Joseph's son Vittorio took mandolin lessons at the French consul's and flirted with his daughter, Lila Laffont. They sang French songs in the moonlight, floating in the waters by the pier of the Mandraki. He studied at a school of French Catholic priests, later, at a lycée in Paris; he remembers the Dreyfus Affair, and speculates on whether Lamartine and Chateaubriand, who are known to have visited Rhodes, might have made a purchase at H.B.'s shop.

With branches in Izmir, Mersin, Adana, and Athens, and offices in Milan and Manchester, Salomon Alhadeff Fils, which was, so the family maintains, the main commercial and banking firm in the Middle East, controlled 90 percent of the economy of Rhodes, the export of cotton, sesame, and figs. The company was split when my grandfather Haco left to set up his own company. Later, the two factions were reunited briefly, but after Salomon's death, and a great deal of strife of the kind families specialize in, they split again. Lots were drawn and the original building went to my grandfather Haco. The two brothers competed against one another shamelessly, but now the competitors are dead and their fortunes no longer fabled: money is abstract, and when it goes, leaves little trace. Having once had money counts for nothing in actual monetary terms, though the memory of money can certainly poison the pleasure of being without it, for several generations. So it was that I inherited what is left of the family fortune—a propensity to live beyond my means.

Rebecca had no manners but she was quick and she was religious: if she discovered there was pork in something she had eaten, she would throw up. She had a passion for tortellini and in Montecatini, where she once went to lose weight, she ate so many—if only she'd known there was ham in the stuffing—she weighed ninety kilos when she got there and a hundred and twenty when she left. Haco fell in love with her beautiful hands and feet, my father maintains.

Nissim believes his father went to Izmir because he couldn't find a wife in Rhodes. He saw Rebecca, fell for her, went to dinner at her father's house, closed the deal. She had never left Izmir. He was twenty-nine or thirty, had a big gold watch chain, had traveled the Mediterranean buying and selling flour, sugar, wood, spices—he inspired awe and he was a catch.

He went to the best photographer in Izmir, asked him to make a full-length portrait of his fiancée and send it to Rhodes by boat, then he went home and told his mother, "My future wife will be here in a week." All week long, his mother made frantic preparations for the coming of the fiancée. Haco went to meet the boat and returned with the life-sized photograph; he thought it a very big joke that his mother had worked baking sweets, airing linens, for the coming of an effigy.

Haco and Rebecca had a regiment of boys, six, and two girls, one of whom died. He was never there when she gave birth, hating to see her suffer. The afternoon Rebecca went into labor for the last time, her three younger sons were banished to the garden: Nissim held Moisé's ears, Moisé held Boaz's ears, and Boaz held Nissim's ears so they wouldn't hear their mother's shrieks. Jacques and Silvio must have been at work. At last, the nanny came out, bearing a very red ten-pound baby, my father, who was named Shalom, though his eponymous grandfather swore he would change it.

The first picture of him: a creature with lustrous auburn curls in a white crochet dress to just below the knees, and a long gold chain hung with amulets: the number thirteen in green vermeil, turquoise stones, gold coins, coral horns, scarab beetles, semiprecious stones. Large green eyes shadowed by black lashes. Hands at the sides. Fluffy painted clouds in the background of the photographic studio. That age when a baby is feminine whether a boy or a girl because in the realm of women.

On one of the family's summer trips to Izmir, my father, who was five, went into the garden to pee and was stung on the bottom by a bee; his brothers quickly put some urine and earth on the spot to alleviate the sting. The six brothers and one sister delight in scatological details. My father is always reminded by his aunt Rachel not to be too grand since she saw his balls when he was a baby.

The first house was in Brussali, and overlooked the open sea. The wind whistled through the windows. There were cauliflowers in the orchard and when the children came home from school, waiting for tea, they would eat the stalks left in the ground after the flower had been cut. The gardener Kristophi was devout. On Sundays, one of the brothers, Moisé, took to shouting down his chimney pipe, "Kristophi, have you prayed?" and Kristophi believed it was the voice of the Lord. He lived from Sunday to Sunday in an exalted state but he could be practical, too: once he got an abscess on his leg and healed it by putting warm cow dung on it until it exploded.

On Saturdays, Haco would pick the children up at school and take them on a picnic. He brought a Persian rug and a watermelon that he put in a fountain of water from a mountain source to cool and they ate brown eggs, pastries, and a chicken cooked in butter and oil that Rebecca had prepared. If she said, "Haco, the food is good," he knew he should wipe his chin.

A Turkish client came to dinner and at the end of the meal, the maid brought bowls of water with jasmine blossoms floating in them. The Turk, who didn't know the water was to rinse his fingers, drank from the bowl and Haco immediately did the same so as not to embarrass him.

He became agent for a Bulgarian shipping company and in 1934 took the family on a free cruise from Rhodes to Alexandria, then Istanbul, through the Bosporus, across the Black Sea, ending up in Varna, south of Sofia. Nissim had a blister on his foot and they went to see the silversmith uncle in Constantinople who talked only of his cataracts and of the operation and how the surgeons had cut; he gave vivid details. Nissim thought he would faint, but he caught sight of a beautiful Czech woman almost twice his age and revived.

Their second house, on the Mandraki, was part of an estate belonging to a Turkish widow called Zyeneb Hanoum, who lived there with her two eunuchs, two sons, and two daughters. The eunuchs cooked and cleaned. Little by little, the widow ran out of money and sold pieces of her property to Haco till she had sold it all and had to go live elsewhere.

The sons were called Ambera and Vehand. Ambera was very agile. He would run for thirty or forty meters, then throw a long bamboo pole in between the bars of my grandfather's gate. Nissim and his brother Silvio were impressed. They took a bamboo cane and cut it. Silvio threw it first and hit Nissim near the eye. Nissim was given a tetanus shot and stayed up all night in a fever. Another time, Nissim was riding a bicycle in front of the house, around the basin. His brothers spat at him from a balcony. He ducked to avoid the spits and ended up in the basin.

Haco gave a party for the new governor of Rhodes. Rebecca and his three sisters made the preparations. One of these sisters had legs each as wide as another person's three legs put together. Every time Rebecca went to market, she returned with another dozen plates. There were twenty-four dozen coffee cups in the house. Two tents were set up in the garden with a covered corridor between them; there was an orchestra and dancing.

The children went to the Alliance Française Israélienne in the Jewish quarter that had been founded by a Rothschild. The discipline, consisting of ten blows on the hands, was more impressive than either the education or the Turkish toilets. They were taken to school in a carriage pulled by a horse called Coty who could only go forward. Everyone in town knew that if they ever encountered him on a narrow road it was they who would have to back up.

The children would awake at five, wrap themselves up in carpets against the morning chill and study till seven. For breakfast they had slices of bread and butter and Rebecca would dip strips of buttered bread in her coffee and give them some. Moisé liked to put butter in the holes in the bread.

They came home at about four, had tea, then studied again till seven. Once a week they had a Turkish bath; on the remaining days they washed sketchily. At seven-thirty Haco came home and one of the boys, usually Nissim, would take his shoes and socks off and put his feet in a basin of hot water. Then, when dinner was ready, he would dry his father's feet and bring him slippers.

They had a cow, milk from the cow, and cream off the top of the milk, but only Haco could touch that. There was a pantry where Rebecca stored dried apricots in a box. The brothers would help themselves to the apricots, then rearrange them to make the box seem fuller than it was.

They studied till eleven and slept, two boys to each room, except for my father, the youngest, who slept with his parents.

In the summer, they went rowing, then to the beach at ten. They had to be home by twelve-thirty and Haco was there to see that hours were kept. At twelve, he would appear on the beach and wave a white handkerchief: that was their signal to come out of the water. After lunch, Haco had a nap and took one of the boys to lie awake next to him so the remaining ones couldn't make too much noise while he slept.

The Mandraki, which the house overlooked, was and is the main promenade in Rhodes. At sundown, people strolled up and down to see and be seen. It was once a veritable marriage market when ships from South Africa docked and disgorged young men who had gone there to make a living and now returned to their island just long enough to find a wife.

At five in the afternoon, the older boys got dressed and went walking up and down the Mandraki until a girl looked back and they would arrange to meet under a tree. Sarah, who was the second child, was not allowed out but watched the proceedings from behind the gate. Like her mother, she was not allowed to visit hospitals or cemeteries. When she insisted on going to a party, her father would escort her. She was not permitted to dance more than twice with the same partner, and if she thought she was about to be asked a third time, she would request to be taken home so as to avoid her father's inevitable rebuff. Then he would say slyly, "I told you these are silly affairs!"

Jacques, the eldest, was a Don Giovanni though because he had a complex about his chest he never swam or even went to the beach. But he wore glasses long after he had stopped needing them—only with neutral lenses—because he thought they gave him an air. He would come home and put on his pajamas, then holler for his younger brothers to go across the street and get him a bottle of cologne. This happened every four or five days since he consumed great quantities of *pisciada,* as he called it, and he was Alegra Abuaf's best customer. (She was

88

later deported and died in a concentration camp.) One day, the brothers, fed up with running their brother's errands, took an empty bottle and peed into it: between them, they did not quite manage to fill it to the brim; still, they wrapped it carefully and brought it to him and only confessed to their prank when he was about to splash some of the contents on his face.

Haco had a correspondent in Marseilles and asked him to find a French tutor for his children. A frail old woman called Mademoiselle Gillet arrived. The brothers were so impervious to any regime more clement than their father's that before long she was relegated to the sewing. She lost fifty needles on the floor of her room and in Rhodes it was believed that if you stepped on one it would pierce your skin and go straight to your heart. One night, the brothers went to her room while she was in the bathroom; one hid under her bed, the other behind the night table. Mademoiselle Gillet entered the room and turned off the light. Moisé grabbed her ankle and when she tried to switch the light back on a hand pushed hers away. She ran out of the room hollering, "A ghost! *A ghost grabbed my foot!*" She left after three months.

But Haco did not give up on the idea of giving his children a cosmopolitan education: Sarah was sent to school in Paris, and Nissim to Aix- en-Provence, before an Italian school was established in Rhodes. That was where my father went, along with his two brothers Boaz and Moisé, and where he learned to wear a black shirt and hat, and to extend his right arm in a fascist salute. He climbed up the Duce's paramilitary ladder: at first, he was a wolf's cub, then a *balilla*, then, at the age of thirteen, he became an *avanguardista*. When the racial laws were passed, no one had heard of concentration camps yet but some ships carrying German Jews supposedly to Palestine had already docked in Rhodes. Although Jews could not hire servants, the maids kept coming to the house, wearing hats so that in case of a sudden inspection by the police they could say they were visiting.

My father remembers feeling afraid, paying attention to what was being said. On one hand, he was still under the influence of the fascist movement; on the other, he was a dirty Jew. "At that age," he said, "you think you're the shit—that everyone is right and you are wrong." Haco and his family left Rhodes in disgrace. They left for Alexandria, where fascist laws were not applied, given the economic force represented by the Jewish community.

The virtues my grandfather Haco is known for are parsimony, an attachment to duty, decorum, the building of a reputation, and of patrimony—capital, whether in the form of bank accounts, shares, or real estate. These "virtues" I did not inherit. As soon as I have two dollars, I spend them both. I have what we call in the family hands with holes in them. But then history has not proved me so wrong. What parades as profligacy on my part may be a crooked wisdom. Fortunes were amassed on both sides of the family, and on both sides they were lost, usually by a member of the family. My grandfather Haco, who saved his pennies from the time he was a young boy, lived long enough to see his eldest son appropriate the fortune he had accumulated. When he went into business and banking he made money in the famously fast, standard, way of making it: charging interest on capital; charging on goods according to demand rather than according to their value, or what had been paid for them. He ordered shiploads of beans, for instance, paying five cents a pound for them and selling them for a dollar. Now, if one is unable to reason so, one does not make money unless one can make something whose value is enigmatic and eludes computation.

My grandfather owned a great deal of real estate in the center of Rhodes. My father estimates that it was worth about five or six million dollars. When the racial laws were passed and suddenly Jews in Rhodes were not allowed to send their children to school, to employ servants, or to speak any language other than Italian, my grandfather, unlike others, more optimistic than he, who waited to see what would happen and lost their lives at it, immediately decided to leave with his family for Egypt. He left his affairs and holdings in the hands of his eldest son Jacques, in one letter, and in another annulled the terms of the first.

Jacques was married to a Turkish Jew by the name of Batami. They had a son, Isidore. In 1943, the Germans deported all the Jews of Rhodes but Jacques bribed the Turkish consul and was able to obtain a Turkish passport. So they were not on the famous ship of Jews bound for concentration camps in Poland and Germany and of which only a handful survived. But the German command soon realized they had been duped and they informed Jacques that he would have to report every day to see if another boat had docked that could deport him and his family. He did so for a year. The ship never did arrive. By then, Rhodes was isolated by a siege of British submarines. The islanders were dying of hunger, and the Germans finally allowed any who wished to sail for Simi. A caïque was filled with refugees, among them Jacques and his family. Just as it reached shore, it sank. From there, the family traveled to Egypt.

My father said, "Every evening he died at the thought of being deported the next day; every morning he lived again when he was told the boat hadn't come." He maintains that the torment Jacques suffered, having agreed to stay behind and supervise his father's possessions, made him feel entitled to them. By the end of the war, they had become his, and so, his son's. It is not clear to what degree this son, now keeper of the family fortune, knows what his father is accused of, but he certainly misses no opportunity to send a gift, or extend an invitation to one or another of his relatives. His father died years ago, and if anyone is responsible, then he was, and the sins of the father are not to be visited on the sons . . . or was it the other way around?

With all my grandfather's painstaking effort at building a career and capital, by the end of his life there was little to encourage one to save money, or to accumulate it. The message seemed to be, rather: spend it while you can.

When the "thief" of the family fortune, Batami, came to Strada in Chianti in August 1991, Aunt Sarah informed us: "She took all that was ours and now she wants to see how I live. She inspected every corner of my house. Didn't leave anything out. Maybe she wants that, too. But you know what bothers me most? It's that face of hers. Like a wet cat. You know what a cat's eyes look like when you pull it out of the water? Like that. That's how she's looked for thirty years. I feel sorry for her."

Sarah had arrived to have coffee with us. She was wearing a shirtdress. The print was a black outline of roses; the shoulders were slightly padded; the inside trim of the collar and front was bright red and it was this detail that lent the dress distinction.

She wore two rows of pearls, her usual bands of rubies, sapphires and diamonds around the ring finger.

I remarked that she was very thin. "It's my colitis," she volunteered, "one day of colitis, one day of eating nothing, one kilo gone."

What substance will harm her is a subject of continuous speculation and conversation. One day it's green beans, the next it's tomatoes. I noticed her high cheekbones, her forehead which is narrower than her cheekbones, that there was little flesh on her face, the long straight nose, blue-grey eyes, the hint of rose make-up, lipstick the color of a rose petal, manicured but unlacquered nails, the long generous hands.

I brought a gold lacquer Japanese tray, with two espressos, a little drop-shaped china dish with five oatmeal biscuits in it. Her eyes glistened for a moment as she picked up a biscuit, delicately. "What is this?" she asked, in a mixture of gratitude and reproof. My mother, never shirking from the utmost truth, answered, "I bought them in Paxos." A month had gone by, one thought instantly, they could be stale by now.

After a little pause: "I am wearing the same thing I wore for John's wedding, on Saturday night," she announced, carefully refraining from telling us what that was, since we had not attended that affair and could therefore still be taken by surprise. She has the exquisite and timely elegance of the woman "who has nothing to wear"—silk dresses in black and white, or bold turquoise and emerald green that make her eyes glow in her face like animate gems. She wears low-heeled black pumps, but by the distortion of her toes it is clear she must have worn, for many decades, narrow, high-heeled shoes. On the subject of shoes, her father would take hers away so she would not be able to go out, and *out*, in the Sephardic citadel on Rhodes, was a protected enclave where everyone knew everyone else.

I walked her to the gate. "Your mother seems much better," she said, lowering her voice, "we'll just have to get adapted to this . . . What do you want to do?" *"Qu'est-ce que tu veux faire?"* in the family lexicon, does not so much mean "What do you want to do?" as "Nothing can be done about it."

She crossed the road to where she always parks her car to avoid coming out of our blind driveway, where she was once hit by a car. She got into her white Renault 5, fastened her seat belt, started the car slowly, reversed, then ventured out onto the road, a hesitant bug.

Sarah was brought up as a woman who should stay in her place in a patriarchal society secretly ruled by women, and was never accustomed to revealing her intentions clearly. Her existence is ostensibly dedicated to the other, whoever that may be—men first, family at large second. Then, holding one in the spell of her radiant servility and acquiescence, she does as she pleases. She may appear to sway graciously like a lily on a stalk to others' suggestions, be interested, flattered, practically persuaded, but, at the last minute, an unforeseen circumstance makes it impossible for her to do anything other than what she had, from the first, envisioned.

Sarah, and my father, are islanders who observe the conventions of how a woman speaks and how a man speaks to uphold the mask they were assigned at birth: he uses it to hide weakness and she to hide strength. When they arrive, there is a radiance about them. They are charismatic, if by that I mean a certain quality that makes others *turn towards* them, which after all, in human contact, is half the battle. And the brother and sister, so much alike—tall, handsome, silvery hair and fluorescent eyes, beholding any who approach with rapt concentration, an intimate ardor that says, "There is no one here but you and me, I have all the time in the world, nothing is more important than you, I will help you if it is in my power"—go about charming the woman in the vegetable store, the cabdriver, the cleaning lady, the carpenter. They have their mother in their blood: once a week, on Rhodes, the poor lined up in Rebecca's kitchen and she distributed rice, flour, sugar, coffee, and oil.

Nissim may rarely speak of his year in concentration camp, but though prosperous, he has a horror of waste—when they have tickets for the theatre, he will drive into Manhattan and be there an hour and a half before the performance in order to find a free parking space. He lives in unconscious fear of destitution. As a teenager, when he was given money to go to the movies, he would go to the theater, look at the pictures on the marquee to see what the film was about, then go home, the money still in his pocket. Like father, like son.

"Oh, fly first class, for God's sake," he was once told by my mother, who has always had a greater interest in creature comforts than in possessions—though what is hers she will not easily relinquish. This is proof of an extraordinary will after forty-five years with my father, who would give his most cherished possessions to the first person that happened to remark favorably on them. Once, he insisted that she give her ivory toiletries set with her grandmother's silver monogram to a Japanese gentleman who had commented on their beauty and with whom my father had business dealings. My mother stalwartly refused.

My much maligned aunt Batami came for cocktails. She turned down a glass of wine and accepted a Sprite and one Japanese cracker wrapped in rice paper, but not a second. She was somewhat stooped, and the back of her blue and white heavy silk jacket was raised where she had a slight hump. Her eyes were more like those of a turtle than those of a cat. She emanated a stillness as though her entire being had been pushed into a very small box, locked up, and the key thrown away. Her only moment of liveliness was when we came indoors and I played Glenn Gould's recording of the Goldberg Variations. She talked about her piano playing: "Do you know Cortot, but maybe you're too young to remember . . . I studied with him in Geneva. I used to hold concerts in Rhodes for one, even two pianos—in those days there was nothing there . . ."

In his less forgiving moods, my father sees Batami as the widow of the black sheep of the family because when he demanded the brothers' share of the inheritance, Jacques replied, once, that he would kill himself, and another time, that he would make trouble for Sarah in Alexandria, where she was already having to report to the police every day and her house and possessions were impounded. One version has it that all the brothers were paid back in cash at the time, Jacques having also offered them the alternative of real estate. They were all sorry now, explained one brother, because had they chosen the real estate their inheritance would have been worth a great deal more. My father scoffed at this version.

The older faction of the family fared better. My grandfather's cousins, principally Vittorio and his brother, expanded, opened a textile factory in Athens and a big office in Milan, but when the racial laws came, they sold the factory, left Milan, and opened a branch in Buenos Aires, in 1939. They made a fortune once again. They opened a trading office, then a textile factory in Argentina. During the revolution, they had two bodyguards and they lost about four million dollars. Still, it was like a drop of water in the sea to them.

Now in his nineties, Vittorio has shrunk: he seems a little man, which I am certain he never was. His goatee is clipped in the shape of an arrow pointing downward; quite large ears and nose, sharp eyes behind glasses; he dresses carefully in the style of European gentlemen of his time—perfumed tailoring. There is charm and quickness, and just below a certain rabbinical interest in the "other," there is the banker, lawyer, merchant, and gaucho. Most men of the family fit this description—he has it undiluted by the uncertainties of the modern condition.

My aunt Sarah had liked her cousin Vittorio in Rhodes. He had asked for her hand, or thought of doing so, but my grandfather put a stop to the courtship. It was resumed some fifty years later, in New York, at the wedding of one of Sarah's nephews. Sarah was then well over seventy, still a beauty. Vittorio was almost ninety, widowed, in the company of a couple in his employ—a chauffeur and a housekeeper.

Sarah continued her peripatetic existence, from daughter to daughter, and brother to brother, but added Buenos Aires to her circuit. More and more suitcases were packed in her little house in Strada in Chianti, and dispatched with her to Vittorio's house. "That country is so far away," she complained of Argentina, "it's like having your back to the wall." No one "passed through" Buenos Aires. You had to have a reason to go there. An Alexandrian, she rebelled at being decentralized.

The family thrived on the romance though from the very start, Sarah struggled with the loss of independence, finding other names for it. The place was a bit backward, she said; it was like Egypt forty years ago, only not so nice; women had nothing to do, they were surrounded by servants; certain members of the family did nothing but bicker among themselves. And some of them were reactionary. She told a woman one day that she found it disturbing to think that there were people living nearby who had neither a toilet nor electricity. "You wouldn't be a communist, by any chance?" the woman said. "Why communist?" Sarah countered. "Is it communist to take an interest in others?"

Around the time of her third or fourth journey, Vittorio provided her with her own telephone line and fax, made little improvements on her room, so that she would be lured into staying, and staying longer. Perhaps he had sensed that she would be a fugitive. "You have gilded my cage," she said, but tried nonetheless to get into the spirit of things. If she was going to remain, then she wanted to participate in the affairs of the house. She started accompanying Vittorio's valet on his errands. The man resented the supervision. There was far too much dishwashing liquid being purchased, Sarah thought: could it be a dishwashing-liquid smuggling ring? In the early afternoon, when everyone had sunk into their daily siesta, she said she saw containers of the precious substance leaving the kitchen, being conveyed to a car.

Once Vittorio sent for his man to come and play a game of cards with him—something they often did. The man sent back the reply that he was watching television. Vittorio was offended and did not ask again. During the showdown, when it came, between Sarah and Vittorio's valet, she was accused of mistrusting him, accused also of turning Vittorio against him. The valet denied any wrongdoing. But the last straw was that Vittorio, when summoned to arbitrate the argument, did not take sides. Her suspicions were probably less interesting to him, given the increasing frailties of age, than remunerated service he could count on. He remained silent and Sarah took the opportunity of withdrawing from the idyll. She announced her departure, then finding no flights for a fortnight, proceeded to spend the remainder of her time in her room. Vittorio fell ill; the doctor had to be summoned in the middle of the night. He was appealing to her sympathy, but it was too late.

The portraits of his late wife, Reniulka, stared down from the walls of the apartment—Sarah had found their continued presence a sign of insensitivity towards her and Reniulka's spirit wafting in the delicate ornateness of the apartment had irked her.

Sarah was not the first to almost end up in Argentina. "After Nissim returned from the camps," she said, "your father thought of going to Buenos Aires. It's a good thing he didn't go. That side of the family were not like us . . ." My father was trying to get out from under his father's rule. He was one of six brothers working for him. What prospects could he have? Ascher, Vittorio's brother, offered him work and obtained a visa for him and my mother. Vittorio himself had been a member of the Fascist party in Italy and as a result of his thesis on the jurisdiction of Rhodes, had even had a private audience with Mussolini. He arrived at Chigi Palace wearing the requisite black shirt and stopped five steps before the entrance to the Duce's office, as instructed by protocol. In religious concentration, the Duce worked at his desk. A beautiful young woman in green trousers and a white cotton blouse was sculpting a bust of him and from time to time interrupted her work to measure his nose, brow, chin, then quickly returned to the modeling clay. Mussolini worked, paying no heed. After about ten minutes, he beckoned to Vittorio to approach. Vittorio did so, thinking it the longest and most embarrassing distance he had ever had to cover, and gave the fascist salute. After questioning him closely on the Dodecanese, Mussolini offered Vittorio a diplomatic post, which Vittorio refused for family reasons, though he accepted a signed photograph of the Duce.

My father decided to convert for practical reasons—Argentina was under fascist rule—and he converted essentially because he was a Jew: had he not been one, there would have been no fear of persecution, no uprooting to begin with. The reasons for the conversion are Jewish; the very term "conversion" is Jewish by nature, implying as it does the power of adaptability from one place, language, currency, to another. It is what has contributed in making Jews the force that they are: *their ability to convert* while remaining separate.

My father was essentially converting from not going to temple to not going to church. His father believed that you could pray from anywhere, even from your own room. He took the family to temple once a year at Rosh Hashana for only one hour. When he became a Catholic, my father dedicated that one hour to going to Mass on Christmas Eve. He said he thought the Jewish religion with its "eye for an eye and a tooth for a tooth," tough, and preferred the Christian turning of the other cheek. As for race, he knew as well as anyone that there is no converting either to or from it.

I V

Nissim was captured by the Germans in Rome, where he had studied medicine: "I am grateful for the discipline I received from my father. Without it, I don't think I would be alive now. I made do with little. The first year in Rome, I lived at the Casa dello Studente. For 500 lire a month, I could eat, sleep, and take girls to the movies. There were twelve volumes of a textbook on anatomy—that alone cost 350 lire. My father's correspondent in Rome used to give me 100 lire every now and then to buy books. I didn't like to spend that money. At the end of the year I had saved 1,000 lire. I wanted a Lambretta badly but even at the third or fourth year of medicine I was still debating the question, 'Shall I buy a Lambretta or shall I buy a coat?' In the end, I bought a coat.

"I obtained my degree in gynecology in July 1942 in Rome. Italy was at war so it was impossible to travel and I was cut off. I managed: I did house calls for an insurance agency. But in October 1943, prompted by Hitler, the fascists in the north proclaimed the Salò Republic, the king went to Egypt, and it was announced that General Badoglio, who had signed an armistice with the Allies, was a traitor. That is when they started to hunt down Jews in Italy.

"I was under the protection of Mrs. Mancia, the mother of a medical student who had been a friend of mine until by some carelessness in the course of an experiment with the typhoid virus, he contracted the infection and died within forty-eight hours. His mother practically adopted me. She was what is known as a Black Catholic—attached to the Pope by her underpants. Through her connections in the clergy, I and another friend were able to hide at the Vatican. We were meant to be on a spiritual retreat. They would wake us at five. Then, what with the novenas, the masses, and the rosaries, after fifteen days I said, I'm not staying here, I'd rather die. Already as a Jew, I didn't believe in anything; I thought, how can I go into a whole other religion . . . Nine months at the Vatican and I would have been ready to enter a lunatic asylum. My friend Luigi Meschieri said, 'I talk with God, I like to, but not all day long—the monotony of it!' We'd been through six years of medical school together.

"We had to get up at five because the priests said that if you stay in bed you get evil thoughts. You know why you get evil thoughts? Because when your bladder is full you get an erection. Whereas if you wake up at five with a cold shower and a rosary, the evil thoughts go away. There were prayers before breakfast, Mass, a sermon, the reading of holy books, the only ones permitted there—the life of Christ, Saint Thomas Aquinas—I liked him, though, so logical, in high school I had written an essay on him.

"Mrs. Mancia came to the rescue again. She took us to Piazza Santa Maria Maggiore, to the Istituto Russico, the Russian monastery. On the other side of the piazza was a hotel called Capitale. At the Russian monastery, I never went out. Some didn't see the sun for nine months. Still, it was a treat to be there. There was a Greek Jesuit with whom I discussed philosophy. Then I could always go and talk to the nuns in the kitchen. After ten days, my university friend left to go and hide at his parents' house. I stayed with the Jesuit. When the doorbell rang, we would go and hide through a trapdoor in the ceiling that you couldn't see from the outside. One night, at about ten, the doorbell rang. I got out of bed, put on my dressing gown, and started walking quietly with the others towards the hiding place when a priest accosted me and said, 'Doctor, one of your fellow Jews collapsed from shock and has lost consciousness.' I went back to see to the man. When I got to his room, I saw that he was bleeding from the nose and from the ear. I diagnosed a cranial fracture. Today you could operate, but at the time there was nothing to be done. I told the priest, 'Padre, you have to take him to the hospital, there is nothing I can do for him.' In fact, the man died shortly after. But just then, a famous pro-Nazi officer called Koch arrived on the scene. He asked me, 'What are you doing here?' In spite of the assurance with which I answered, he did not believe me. I saw that it was all over. I was arrested along with two others who had been drinking, as they did every night, and had never even heard the doorbell.

"In the van, an officer asked Koch, 'Where shall we take them?' Koch replied, 'Take them to the Villa.' I was reassured; I thought, 'A villa, how bad could that be?' 'The Villa' was jargon for the prison of Regina Coeli. There, my fingerprints were taken and I was put in a cell with two others.

"We had a bucket that was emptied once a day. At the beginning I felt awkward about it, but one of my mates, who was Jewish though pretending not to be, having even changed his name to Amedeo Cristiano, said, 'Nissim, don't worry. Do what you have to do, then we'll burn a sheet of newsprint and the smell will go away.'

"I would sit at the window and look out at the house across the street. I knew how to communicate by sign language—nearly everyone at school did so as to pass information during exams—and that is how I communicated with my girlfriend when she left home to go and buy bread at six in the evening. One day, I saw a young woman and signed to her to get in touch with my mate's wife, who didn't know that he was in jail, and with Mrs. Mancia.

"After ten days, Amedeo, whose real name was Spizzichino, was freed because they saw him praying constantly; they were convinced he must be Catholic. I stayed another ten days. Mrs. Mancia brought me some oranges. It was the beginning of February. My girlfriend told me that they would be taking me up north and she brought me a hat and a beautiful camel hair coat. *Se me fué de los ojos:* I never enjoyed it. I think an SS officer took it. The hat was taken at Auschwitz. Four days before the incident of the Ardeatine Caves where about 335 Italians, one-fourth of them Jews, were killed by Germans in retaliation for 32 German soldiers killed, I was taken to Fossoli di Carpi. A nurse I had met in Rome came to see me. She went to the sergeant in charge and told him she knew me, that I was a doctor, a nice man who had never hurt anybody and that I should be released. She hadn't understood yet . . ."

"I was deported from Rome chained like a common criminal. In Fossoli, near Modena, the Germans were amassing Jews from all parts of Italy. It seemed they weren't rounding up many, since a month went by between one load and the next. I spent a tranquil month there as the SS wanted the Italians around us to think they were conscientious and compassionate, that they respected basic human rights. I was even allowed to practice medicine; in fact, I was forced to amputate the leg of one prisoner, which had frozen and developed gangrene during the journey from Rome to Fossoli. The SS saw to the meticulous maintenance of the camp's living quarters. Anyone who wished could have a medical checkup, one a day even, and ask for any treatment, especially revitalizing ones, which were the most popular. Some considered themselves almost lucky to have been caught and to be allowed such calm, safe days, instead of a freedom marred by the fear of being apprehended, and of having to beg a new hiding place every night. But more and more people arrived—of all ages and conditions. The dormitories filled up and became overcrowded; we felt that our stay in Fossoli would soon be over. There were rumors aimed at raising our spirits and making our imminent departure acceptable. We knew nothing for certain; we had heard that we would be going to Poland, to cities that were wholly Jewish, where we would be allowed to practice a profession without fear of being persecuted. Most of us entertained these notions in the hope that a final resolution might be in sight, that the continual transfers from prison to camp, and from camp to camp, might be at an end. One morning, as some applied for a checkup and others found fault with their vitamin treatments, the order was given for our departure on the following day, at dawn."

"We left not knowing our destination, or how we would travel; we abandoned whatever friendships and habits we had adopted in that brief time. The future was uncertain. The Germans spread rumors that were optimistic and disastrous by turns so as to raise our hopes and our fears; they did it to undermine our confidence. That night, no one slept. The number of guards around the fences had been tripled, though hardly anyone thought of escaping. As if aware of our destiny, we tried to leave to the lucky few, who were racially mixed either by marriage or by birth, a letter or a testament to be delivered to loved ones on the glorious day of liberation.

"That night seemed eternal; we believed it would be our last in the world as we knew it. When dawn came, life had stopped smiling for all 620 of us. Instinct, which is often superior to intelligence, told us so. It was a misty dawn: our names called in alphabetical order by the rasping voice of the marshal of the SS resounded like a death sentence. Without a word or a hint of rebellion, we started towards the truck headed for the train station. Everything was handled with the greatest possible precision and speed. At the station, we were crammed into cattle cars, thirty-five to fifty of us at a time. With a little skill we could have escaped but no one did so because the SS had told us that for every man missing, ten would be shot. If I had to do it over again, I wouldn't hesitate to run, even if it meant that more than ten men would be shot in retaliation, knowing it would be an act of charity towards both myself and those executed.

"There were about fifty of us in one rather confined car. Not all had room to sit. We took turns, giving older people and women precedence. There were no children, fortunately. I was half-sitting in a corner when the door was shut from the outside and the train started its tragic march. No one spoke; we understood the seriousness of the moment. I looked around: I wondered what they wanted with that eighty-year-old man and the woman who assisted him. And the man with the white hair, the bruised eyes, and bruises everywhere—what had he done?

He came from the prison of San Vittore in Milan, where a captain of the SS had mistreated Jews in a way I did not yet comprehend. And the unfortunate man whose leg I had amputated, what work could he do? Of what possible use could he be to the great Reich? And the elegant lawyer, still upset that he had soiled his clothes leaning on the side of the convoy, afraid to bend his knees in case it would ruin the crease in his trousers. And all those young girls, especially one whose hands were clearly more accustomed to wearing jewels than to working—she was huddled on the floor like a rag, her beautiful blond hair matted. Ignorant of her fate, she smiled sadly; I wish she could at least have kept that smile when, thin as a rail and worn down by work and hunger, tired of life at the age of twenty, she asked to be interned in one of those hospitals that were a waiting room to cremation ovens."

"The train sped on, making very few stops. The Germans seemed in a hurry to cross the Italian border; surveillance was very strict; once we were on Austrian territory, it let up a little. At midnight, we reached the Brenner Pass. After that, we felt completely isolated from the outside world, since we didn't speak German. The next morning, just before Innsbruck, the train stopped. We were allowed to get off to satisfy our bodily needs, as long as we stayed near the train. It was a harrowing spectacle. All modesty and reticence were cast aside, and the animal instinct made it hard to distinguish between men and women. The spectacle was to repeat itself several times.

"At Innsbruck, we were left for ten hours on an abandoned track. We were not hungry and the meager ration of a bun spread with jam proved more than sufficient. We headed towards Munich, and the beauty of the Tyrolean valley only sharpened our sadness. The sight of chalets, steeped in snow and surrounded by trees, their chimneys smoking, made us long for our home and loved ones, and reminded us of what we had become: wretched beings without a fixed place in which to live, or a destination.

"In Munich, we were given hot soup and it restored us somewhat after the long cold journey; nearly all of us had brought provisions from Fossoli but we didn't dare touch them, thinking to keep them for harder times. During the journey, even the guards did not seem to know when we would arrive, or where we were headed. At every station, the conductor was advised of the next station to be reached. And so, after Munich, we reached Prague and stopped there for half a day. When we departed at sundown the city was a phantasmagoria of rosy palaces and golden cupolas. We piled up in front of the openings on the sides of the cattle wagon, anxious to look out, as though sensing it might be the last city we would see for some time.

"We had been traveling for four days and four nights and we were exhausted. Our only wish was to arrive, and amidst hope and regret only one voice was raised in protest; it was the voice of a German Jew who had cut her wrists, and tried to escape in Fossoli: 'I wish this trip would never end,' she said. Having witnessed the first racial persecutions in Germany, she had sought refuge in Italy. We all thought she must be unbalanced; later we understood that she had been the only sane one among us. On the morning of the sixth day, there were rumors that we had arrived. We hurried to look out: what we saw was neither a station nor a town, but a plain that stretched out as far as the eye could see, and almost entirely barren. In the distance, against the rising sun, were the silhouettes of endless lines of prisoners, dragging their feet, being led to work by guards. But we still didn't understand: we thought they were prisoners expiating a life sentence."

"All at once, the doors of the convoys opened. We were asked to get down, leave our luggage to the left of the train, and quickly line up. It was done in a flash. We looked at our luggage yearningly, thinking of the provisions we would never see again. We had been lining up for a while when we were ordered to fall into two groups: one made up of the young and able-bodied—about 140 of us—and the other of invalids, old people, women, children—about 480 of them. Twenty vans had been readied and the 480 piled into them, pushing to get in, as though they believed that to be left behind would mean the irreparable. Every inch was crammed full; young mothers gathered their children to them, happy not to have been separated; feverish invalids smiled, in spite of their uncomfortable position, perhaps imagining a warm bed at the end of their journey; old people put up with anything on condition of being allowed to go on living. No one suspected the end that awaited them. I am quite certain that all those who boarded the vans died. Thinking to take a simple shower, they got undressed, and calmly, a piece of soap in their hand, entered rooms that looked like showers in every respect, when suddenly instead of water, gas filled the stall. They probably didn't even have time to grasp their predicament before they lost their senses. They were the luckiest because they died immediately."

"The vans left quickly, and those on board said goodbye, and that they hoped to see us again soon. We remained on line indifferently, awaiting orders. The women who had been left behind were grouped together by a woman of the SS, and led to a different camp from ours, in Birkenau.

"With two SS in front, two at the sides, and two behind us, we started our slow march. No one spoke, no one was in the mood to do so. I looked at every inscription, every sign, trying to discover where I was. After a few hundred meters, at a track crossing that was a makeshift station, my curiosity was satisfied: on a decrepit sign I read 'AUSCHWITZ.' If I had to leave my bones there, I would at least know where I left them. We continued to walk and after about fifteen minutes, we reached the entrance to the camp. It was surrounded by high and curved wire fences, supported by concrete columns and charged with high-voltage current. The gate was adorned by three small statues that were caricatures of a Jew, a monk, and a deformed man—three types considered harmful to society and therefore to be eliminated. A dwarf eunuch received us, laughing uproariously. He and a doctor of the SS led us to an area between some barracks where we were told to wait. About twenty men turned to the doctor and said that in the confusion they had misunderstood but that they were ill and therefore could not work. They tried to convince him as best they could. He didn't take long to make up his mind: he had the men led out of the camp. I don't know whether they left on foot or by van."

"I should describe how the camps were organized. Auschwitz was made up of a number of one- or two-storey buildings, and every floor was divided into two dormitories. Each building was called a "block" and was headed up by a *Blockältester*: he was, in ninety percent of the cases, chosen from among common prisoners who had distinguished themselves for their cruelty and brutality. This is how the Germans ran camps of one thousand to two thousand prisoners with only three SS, a minimum outlay of personnel. The *Blockältester* could choose two to six men to assist him: he was the absolute authority of the block and could act as he thought best as long as the block was clean and he reported the exact number of prisoners under him to the SS every morning and every evening. Order and cleanliness were the SS's chief concerns, since they feared the spread of contagious diseases. The *Blockältester* took orders from a *Lagerältester*, who in turn received orders from the command führer and coordinated the activities of the various *Block-ältester*s.

"There were other important posts held by prisoners, such as the lager chiefs who supervised labor and new constructions in the camp itself, and distributed newly arrived prisoners according to demand; another important post was that of *Schreiber*, or scribe, responsible for the number of prisoners at the camp, since together with the SS he counted every morning and every evening all the prisoners who left camp to go to work. These posts were coveted, as those chosen to fill them led a princely life—they received extra rations, as much clean underwear as they wanted, and new shoes and clothes, though in keeping with camp uniforms. Two or three pages made up their room, polished their shoes, and were at their disposal as needed. Every two or three days, a block führer would come to inspect the cleanliness of dormitories, and more especially, of lavatories—halls containing a row of twelve toilet bowls each. One could enter them in the morning from seven to eight, and again in the evening from six-thirty to seven-thirty. After every shift, they were cleaned by two prisoners, who then guarded the entrance for the remainder of the day and allowed no one to enter. The prisoners assigned to this detail were strict and their punctuality was rewarded with extra rations of soup.

"It was a spectacle in the morning to see how twelve toilet bowls could be used in one hour by six hundred individuals. There was the lucky man who was already seated, someone in front of him, waiting, and others who waited for those who waited. For the first three-quarters of an hour a certain sense of civility reigned, as those who were taking long were exhorted to hurry up. But as eight o'clock approached, one thought nothing of interrupting someone who had just sat down as he was about to relieve himself, pulling him to his feet and chasing him away. It was essential to be quick; as for the constipated, their life was even grimmer.

"In Auschwitz, there were two or three infirmary blocks for Aryans, and for Jews, too, if they had any work left in them. The doctors were nearly all Jewish and highly qualified, but they had to submit to the orders of common prisoners, more skilled at wielding a knife or a gun than a stethoscope or a scalpel. Sometimes these prisoners discovered hidden medical skills in themselves, and paying no heed to the advice of doctors, diagnosed and invented treatments for patients whose suffering was thus often abruptly curtailed.

"Near Auschwitz, there were two other large camps, Monowit and Birkenau. Birkenau was a mixed camp, divided into separate areas for men and women. Its cremation ovens worked around the clock. The chimneys emitted black smoke and those who came from that camp said that a smell of burnt chicken was constantly in their nostrils. But the most infernal spectacle was when in 1944 a great number of convoys carrying Hungarian Jews arrived. The ovens worked without interruption for about thirty days, day and night. In the black of night, seeing flames light the top of chimneys made the skin crawl. Those who died a more or less natural death were also taken to be burned at Birkenau."

"I now resume my story where I left off. We waited in a space between two blocks, huddled in our heavy coats, trying to find a ray of sun in which to warm ourselves. Up until then, everything had unfolded in a calm and orderly fashion, but all of a sudden three SS appeared leading a group of prisoners, most of them common criminals, who had been assigned to us. Orders started to fly. The three SS each occupied one corner, keeping perfectly still, their guns in full view, and every now and then came to life with a strident, incomprehensible shout. We were ordered to deposit all our money in a box. Some came forward showing a note that had been issued to them by the SS in Fossoli entitling them to receive in marks the value of the lira they had handed over there. A few kicks and punches made them understand that it was best not to insist on that point.

"In another box, we were made to leave our pens and watches. I still had the watch and pen that had accompanied me through school and university. We had spent more than ten years together. The model of the watch was somewhat outdated, and the tip of the pen a little blunted, but I could still write with it perfectly well; these objects evoked my past and made it concrete. Now that I was about to be parted from them, I felt as though they were my last remaining links to life. A strange melancholy assailed me at the thought of losing something which in my present isolation could still be of some comfort to me. I gave a start: almost unthinkingly, I smashed the watch, which stopped ticking, and when no one was looking, I blunted the nib of the pen. I had had my revenge, and from that moment on, I felt completely detached from life, prepared for whatever might happen.

"We lined up in alphabetical order; each of us was given a slip of paper with a number on it. We were asked to roll up our left sleeve and to go stand in front of two prisoners who tattooed the number on the slip of paper onto our arm with pointed pens dipped in a special ink. I was so agitated I barely felt the pain. That number became, from then on, our name and surname; it was with the number that we received our rations, and went to work; it was with the number, tattooed large on the chest, that bodies were thrown into the cremation oven.

"More shocks lay ahead. We were led into a little room in one of the blocks. The shouting and yelling of the SS and their attendants grew more strident, and more frequent, so that we were completely addled. We were ordered to strip, and to bundle up our clothes into our coat neatly. I undressed as quickly as I could, and left my bundle in a visible spot, hoping to recognize it at once when I returned. I had a ring that I took the precaution of hiding in my coat. Others, wiser than I, swallowed their rings, and later had to retrieve them . . . Some coats were lined with bills and gold pounds sterling and were worth a fortune.

"As I walked, dazed and naked, towards another room that was meant to be the shower, I felt my head being grabbed and held against someone's belly. I felt a clipper shear my hair. Recovering from the surprise, I realized it was a barber on a stool doing this. Three or four other barbers performed the same op-

115

eration on others. Calmly allowing myself to be shaved, I thought how sadistic it was of the SS to have sold us combs and brilliantine two days before deporting us. We were taken into the next room and depilated with more or less rudimentary instruments such as hand-held razor blades—and without either water or soap. I need not describe the cuts, the pain, the anxiety. The next step was disinfection: a prisoner who was at least two meters tall, and wore a glove dipped in disinfectant, quickly and skillfully daubed our armpits and crotch, then ran his glove back over our entire body once more. A kick landed us in the shower. This is how the SS safeguarded our health. They wanted those of us who were healthy to remain healthy.

"In the showers, one soap had to be shared by four men, and there had to be forty of us before the water was made to run. There were ten showers, so that each shower had to serve four people at once. The water was sometimes cold, sometimes hot. After three minutes it was cut off. We tried to hurry but it was impossible to wash properly: if the water was running, we didn't have the soap, and if we were lathered, there was no water with which to rinse off, as someone else had already taken our place. Naked, half lathered and half washed, without being allowed to dry off, we were made to run outdoors, cold as it was, across fifty or so meters to another block where we were randomly handed a shirt, a jacket, a pair of pants made of striped blue and white natural fabric, a pair of work socks—swatches of fabric—a pair of wooden clogs, and a cap. Hardly anyone received anything that fit: the trousers were too short on some, the sleeves too long on others, or the shoes too small. Heading towards the quarantine block, we tried to remedy the problem by exchanging the various items among ourselves.

"When we reached the block, we were not allowed to go in,

116

but were left to wait outside for various hours. I was half-seated in a corner, and looking around despondently, when a certain Enriquez, whom I had met in Fossoli, approached me. He was a Jew from Istanbul who had gone to live in Milan for family reasons. He was Middle Eastern in both appearance and mentality. He sat next to me, and in an effort to comfort me, said: 'Imagine that you are sitting in an armchair at La Scala, or some other theater, watching the most comical of spectacles. Who could ever have imagined such a metamorphosis in the lawyer over there, who days ago in Fossoli had been so elegant in his well-pressed suit and flamboyant tie, and now, in a striped uniform that is too small for him, a torn shirt without a collar, and a shaved head riddled with cuts, seems more ragged than a beggar. And that one over there, with all those patches, those shoes like boats, that scarecrow hat—I think it must be the doctor who was always preening like a cock among the pretty women. As for the big fat man, lying with one eye closed and one open, he must be trying with one to get used to this sad reality, while with the other he undoubtedly dreams of plates piled high with steaming spaghetti.' Thus Enriquez tried to raise my morale, and his. Two days later he contracted a serious form of measles, was immediately isolated, and never seen again.

"In the quarantine block, there were, aside from us, about three hundred Belgian Jews and five hundred Russians, saboteurs moreover. Towards evening, large vats were brought in that were filled with a soup consisting largely of water, a few potatoes and turnips, some flour as thickener, and something that looked like fat. For almost a thousand of us, there were no more than a hundred plates. We had to wait for a comrade to finish in order to be served. But either because we were hungry, or because those who arrived last always received the worst

117

helpings, we did not have the patience to wait. Those served first had to swallow the hot soup with all speed, scorching their mouth as they did so. Some did not let go of their plate once they were through until they had wiped it clean with their fingers several times, then with their tongue, to polish off every last drop. There was no water and even if there had been we could not have washed the plates between uses because there was no time. For the first fifteen days, after I had eaten a little I threw up in disgust at the thought of how the plate had been cleaned. I didn't stop eating but went on, only to throw up again a few minutes later. In time I got used to it, and anyone could have done whatever they wanted in my plate, it would not have caused me the least disgust.

"That night we slept two to a bunk that was ninety centimeters wide. It was impossible to lie on one's back. I found a tolerable position: one of us would turn on his side, with his knees bent, and the other would do the same right behind him, facing in the same direction. The only problem was that if one wanted to turn over, he had to wake the other to warn him.

"I remained in quarantine at Auschwitz three weeks. During that time, we were all given medical checkups, and injected with a vaccine compound on two different occasions, as the SS greatly feared infectious diseases. But we had to earn our keep. For every job that needed to be done at the camp—and there were always some—we would be called on first. Among the various possibilities, I preferred doing the laundry. I separated the pants from the jackets, loaded them onto a cart, and took them to the deposit in the washroom. At first, I returned from work feeling very demoralized, having found most of those pants soiled, and not knowing why. I understood later that the doubt and uncertainty was such, when new work convoys were being formed, that many, out of nervousness and fear, became incontinent. The pockets of every jacket, of every pair of pants, had to be minutely searched. If I found a piece of bread in a dead man's pocket, I took it and waited till I was really hungry to eat it—about eight or nine hours later. I found spoons, which were very useful since we didn't have any, and, even more interesting, pencil sharpeners. I handed these over to a friend, who, like me, was a native of Rhodes: with an innate business sense, he traded them for extra bread or soup. It might surprise you that prisoners were willing to sacrifice a part of their ration in exchange for a pencil sharpener when we only received three hundred grams of bread and twenty-five or fifty grams of margarine a day. You could argue that we might as well have eaten the bread and margarine in chunks, not wasting time to spread the margarine and cut the bread. But it would only prove that you don't know what it's like to eat a ration knowing that twenty-four hours will have to go by before you are given another, of the same size. We spread the bread with a veil of margarine, then cut a thin slice of it and ate it very slowly, savoring every morsel. The last slices were transparent, and cut again into small pieces; so we had the impression we were eating more, and that made us feel less hungry. Before cutting the bread, we slipped a sheet of newsprint or fabric under it so that the crumbs would not be wasted and could be had for 'dessert.' The price varied according to whether the sharpener had one blade or two, and to how thick the blade was; and my friend knew how to show off his wares since he was a master at cutting the thinnest of slices when he gave practical demonstrations."

"After three weeks, when we numbered twenty-five hundred, we were divided into groups that would be distributed among the various small camps that were part of Auschwitz. I was assigned to a truck with about fifty other prisoners. Before our departure, we asked a supervisor where we were headed. He answered that we were very lucky because we were going to a camp where the rations were bigger and the work easier: our work would consist of nailing wooden crates. But as I got on the truck my relief evaporated at the thought of all those who had a few weeks earlier boarded a similar truck and never been seen again. I resigned myself to the possibility of ending up in a gas chamber, and instead of being alarmed or despairing, I felt a great calm come over me.

"We arrived at a small camp, about twenty minutes from Auschwitz—Iavishovitz—lugubrious for the blackness of its twenty huts, and even more, for the macabre aspect of its inhabitants. Unlike Auschwitz, where the work was lighter, and the possibility of eluding surveillance greater given the vastness of the camp, in Iavishovitz, the prisoners with their yellowish cast typical of those who hardly ever see the sun, and their extreme emaciation brought on by very hard labor, looked to me like standing corpses. On their long thin neck was planted a skeletal head in which the only signs of life were large sunken eyes, darting about, ready to seize on anything that might be edible. Their thighs were reduced to the size of the femur, and the skin barely covered their bones and almost totally atrophied muscles. The first thing I did was to measure the circumference of my neck and thighs, and from then on, religiously, at least once a week, I repeated the procedure.

"In Iavishovitz we were once again shaved and sheared, and this recurred every fifteen days. Again, we were given cold and hot showers, our clothes were changed, and we underwent a summary physical checkup. Only those who had a weak heart could avoid descending into the mine. Great was the joy of the SS on finding a merchant, or even better, a professional, they could assign to the hardest manual labor. So it was, that on the very next day I embarked on my new and unprecedented career as a miner.

"We took turns so that work in the mine could be continuous. There were three shifts: one in the morning, one at midday, and one at night. We worked for eight consecutive hours, but when there was need for an increased production of coal —which happened very often—we worked twelve or fourteen consecutive hours. To that must be added an hour and a half to reach the work site, and an hour and a half to return to camp, so that we were sometimes on our feet from sixteen to seventeen hours a day, and on our toes, as there was never any lack of surprises.

"I was assigned to the midday shift. We would leave camp at midday, rain or shine. In the summer, we went barefoot so that our shoes might last longer; at first, until the soles of our feet became callused, it was extremely painful to walk, especially on unpaved roads. We were always accompanied by about ten SS, who guarded us at the sides, the front, and the rear. No one was allowed to stray from the file, for any reason. The SS had the right, in fact the duty, to shoot anyone who did so. And it happened that we witnessed tragicomic situations when one of us was suffering from weak intestines.

"Once we reached our destination, the most distressing thing was to descend into the mine. Pushed on all sides, at the risk of being beaten with a stick when we least expected it, we took a lamp, then proceeded quickly into the overcrowded elevator, which swiftly descended to four hundred meters. The first few times, what with the anxiety and the heavy air injected into the galleries by means of a special mechanism, I found it almost impossible to breathe. Once down, we had to walk at length through low galleries full of puddles to reach the work site. We arrived at about two, and were exhausted even before we began. We stopped working at ten at night. We arrived back at camp at about midnight, and every night took a shower, which was mandatory so that we would wash all the coal soot off our skin, allowing the pores to breathe.

"At one, we were given our ration, which consisted of three hundred grams of bread, fifty grams of margarine, and sometimes a piece of salame. We went to sleep at about one-thirty. But that's not all: at least two or three times in the course of the night we would be awakened suddenly, and in all speed would have to line up to be counted. In time, I learned to get up, get in line, and return to bed like an automaton, and often the next morning, couldn't have said precisely how many times I had gotten up.

"We were awakened every day at six-thirty. From eight to eleven we had to work at the camp, cleaning, and helping with new construction. At eleven, we had our soup, which was sometimes thick and edible, but more often watery, with a few potatoes and many turnips in it. On Sundays, a few bits of meat were added, and the unspeakably fortunate few who found a piece of it on their plate would put off eating it, first drinking the liquid, then showing their comrades the minuscule morsels as if they had won the lottery. Every fortnight, we had a Sunday off and those who had worked well would be rewarded with a few cigarettes or a bottle of fizzy water.

"It was on those workless Sundays that we most yearned for

home. They were the saddest days for us. When we worked, our only thought was to return to camp to eat and sleep—there was no time to think. But whenever we had any free time, we remained among ourselves, and in a low voice reminisced about our past, our family and country. We spoke of intimate things as though we found ourselves beyond life and the things of life no longer interested us. But deep down, we felt regret, a longing to resume our habits, or to see a happy or a tragic end to our torture. When memories had made our hearts swell, and each in silence followed his own thoughts, there was always one among us who would suddenly start discussing politics. And we would all be ready, then, to countenance the most fantastic news, the most spectacular offensives, the boldest landings. The so-called experts in our midst would clearly sum up the situation, and with great ease and dexterity, cause entire divisions to advance across hundreds of kilometers; so much so that by the time we got up from these sessions, we were certain that we would be liberated, if not after two weeks, then after a month. This took place punctually every fortnight, and every free Sunday our faltering morale was given a boost, our hopes were renewed, and our faith in the Allies' victory became unshakeable. That faith was undoubtedly our only sustenance and comfort, and we saw how those who had lost it, who had given up hope, were the most likely to lose weight and prepare themselves to be 'selected.'

"The days of selection were days of mourning for the entire camp. A doctor of the SS would come especially to choose those who were wasted and could no longer work profitably. The checkup consisted of stripping naked and showing ourselves front and back. A flattening of forms, denoting that the muscles had become flaccid, was sufficient to land one on the list of the selected. For the most part, forms were not just flattened, they disappeared altogether; bodies grew longer as they became thinner, and it seemed as though the bones would pierce the skin. Future candidates for the cremation ovens were easy to identify: to climb up a step they used both hands to hoist up one leg, then the other. On the day that the SS doctor came to the camp, we would warn those people, begging them not to go to the infirmary. But as though they hadn't heard, they continued to present themselves—I even saw some who voluntarily came to be selected, preferring death to a life that was worse than death. Only those who still had God knows what connection to the outside world tried, during checkups, to appear stronger than they felt, and still capable of hard work. But once their sentence had been pronounced, they no longer rebelled, as though it were their inevitable fate.

"Wearing only a shirt, and barefoot, they were made to board those accursed trucks. The voice of an acquaintance by the name of Barda still resounds in my ears, when he said to me as he climbed onto the truck, '*Vingt-six ans jetés dans un four crématoire*' (Twenty-six years thrown into a cremation oven). We watched them leave without regrets, almost happy for them, thinking of the day when our turn would come. We watched them and they, unlike those first ones, did not bid us farewell or express the hope of seeing us again. They left and their death reminded us of our life, and for several days no one spoke; we withdrew into ourselves, into our grief and forebodings. Work continued, as though nothing had happened, unremitting, merciless.

"The mine took us back, and we forgot the past and the future. The galleries were low—sixty centimeters, to a maximum of a meter and a half. We were constantly having to hoe in the most awkward and uncomfortable positions, trying never to get caught resting by the supervisor. In those low galleries, full of soot, bent on our knees, the air was insufficient, especially if one had to muster a great deal of energy. As soon as the supervisor had gone by, I would throw myself on the ground, allowing my muscles to rest for at least two minutes; I could then resume work with greater courage, anxiously awaiting the supervisor's next round.

"The first day, as soon as I was lowered into the mine, with my rudimentary German, and that of a Frenchman who spoke it quite well, I managed to convey to the civilian miners, who in order to avoid the worst were obliged to work for the Germans, that I was a doctor. After that, they held me in greater esteem, sparing me the heavier tasks, and sometimes helping me. But it was when I treated an eczema that a Polish civilian laborer had long had on his leg that I achieved renown and greater tranquility. We would hide in an abandoned gallery in order not to be seen by the SS on duty, and I would examine him by the light of our lamps. I was very lucky, because the eczema, treated with my prescriptions, began to heal, to the joy and awe of my patient. From then on, every evening, the Pole would summon me into a corner and share his ration with me. These so-called collaborators were very well fed by the Germans, so every day I received twice my usual ration of fat and bread. Not only was I eating, but the Pole obtained that I work under him; as a result, I did almost no work, and enthralled him for hours with descriptions of the Pope's immense riches, his favorite topic since he was a fervent Catholic.

"But this placid life was not to last. My benefactor was transferred to another part of the mine, and though he sometimes sent me things to eat, I went back to working hard, excavating and adapting new galleries. These were full of water; water dripped from the ceiling too and we were always drenched; the work was exhausting because we were constantly drilling into rock. My strength began to fail. The measurements of my neck and thigh had decreased greatly, which further lowered my morale. Whereas before I had remained calm on the days of selection, now I was apprehensive. In spite of the life we led, in spite of the suffering, the hunger, I was in no mood to die; I still had hopes, wishes that had not been fulfilled. I considered following the example of a Jew from Salonika: when he felt he couldn't hold out any longer, he put one finger on the railway track and waited for the little wagon loaded with stones to run over it; then, with blood dripping from the wound, he ran to announce, in a voice that suggested joy rather than pain, that he had had an accident. The finger was amputated, but he was allowed to convalesce for thirty days. I might have done the same, though it took desperate courage, but just then, I developed a miraculous boil on one knee, so big that I couldn't bend my leg. I was hospitalized. The commander of the infirmary, a major of the SS, a cultivated person and the only German I remember with gratitude, took a liking to me, and appointed me undertaker—certainly one of the most coveted posts.

"I worked from six-thirty in the morning till eight in the evening, with a two-and-a-half-hour break at midday and an extra ration of soup. The work was not difficult; it was only a matter of getting used to it. I had to undress the dead, inscribe the number they wore on their arm onto their chest in large letters with a copying pencil, and stack them in piles, ready to be loaded onto trucks that would take them to the cremation ovens. In my free time, I helped in the infirmary, dressing wounds. This was done with paper bandages; I was very good at it, and used only the strict amount of bandage necessary. There was no one who didn't have either a boil or a giant carbuncle. These never healed because they were excised prematurely, and before the wound had a chance to heal, the men would be sent back to work. With the infection still in progress, receiving insufficient nourishment, and working hard, those men were soon reduced to skeletons.

"Only those who dared to be active on the black market could survive, bringing to the mine shirts and leather shoes that the *Blockältesters* had scavenged: in exchange for these, Polish civilians would give liquor, meat, and pork fat. Traders received a few extra rations of bread and soup from the *Blockältester*. But woe to those caught redhanded. Beatings would rain down: seventy to a hundred blows, delivered at full force. I remember the case of one man who was discovered with a bottle of wine: he was beaten unconscious. His body was bruised from the waist down, and in certain places, the raised skin had formed pockets of blood. For three days, he could neither lie nor sit, though he continued to work. This incident didn't stop him from resuming his trafficking after a few weeks. Those extra rations of soup and bread were sufficient to keep him alive and in relatively good health, and he was willing to face any danger to obtain them. On a full stomach, he could at least get some sleep, while most of the others would get up in the deep of night and go wandering about, their eyes starting from their sockets, in search of a crust of bread. Sometimes I, too, woke up but tried to distract myself from the urge to go in search of something I would certainly not find. My favorite distraction was to think of the day when we would be liberated: I remembered, then, all of our collective fantasizing, and began to see big tanks, and parachutists falling from the sky, come to liberate us, while the SS bailed out. Little by little, I fell asleep, continuing to fantasize in my sleep."

"The days passed but we had no exact sense of time. We knew that the front was drawing nearer, as the alarm sirens were becoming more frequent, especially at night. During those alarms every light was turned off and the current in the fences was interrupted. Once, a prisoner took advantage of the pitch dark and managed to escape. He strayed in the countryside for twenty days, stealing clothes and provisions here and there. He was caught and led back to camp. A gallows was erected at the center of the camp and we were made to form ranks all around it. The prisoner, a young man about twenty-five years of age, climbed the few steps up to it with a firm gait; his face blank, he heard out the sentence that condemned him to capital punishment. He looked around at us for a time, then resolutely climbed onto a stool that had been placed before him. He allowed his hands to be tied behind his back, and the noose to be slipped around his neck. Then the executioner, a common prisoner, kicked the stool, and the man hung. A quiver ran through his body, his mouth twitched—that was all. Only the eyes, staring hideously, expressed horror. The body was left to sway late into the night, as a threat and a warning. But soon even this grim episode was forgotten—something much more interesting occupied us: through the German newspapers which entered the camp clandestinely, we surmised that something new was happening on the eastern front. There was talk of a Russian offensive in Kraków and a strange excitement had taken hold of the camp. There were conflicting opinions. We would all be either killed or evacuated; I was of the second opinion, because I believed that as long as the great Reich needed hands, our life would not be in danger. No one thought that they would leave such a sizable workforce to the Russians.

"Amid hope, illusion, doubt, we reached the morning of the eighteenth of January, 1945. At about eight, some of the German rear guard went by; at ten, an endless column of female prisoners began to march past us. They were all young, most of them Jewish, of all nationalities: they smiled and, though it was forbidden, called to us who watched from a distance, asking whether we had news of a loved one. Among them, many were fat, abnormally fat, the sort of awkward fat that is caused by a glandular dysfunction. I found out later that they had been experimentally ovariectomized: we had, before our eyes, human guinea pigs. After two hours, it seemed that the column was at last drawing to a close. The most enfeebled, the eldest, and the thinnest brought up the rear. An emaciated woman in her forties remains etched in my mind: she dragged herself along the icy road, wearing a rope shoe on her left foot and a rough wooden clog on the right one. The wooden clog beat somberly and rhythmically on the ice, but now and then, after the sound of dogs barking, the footsteps became more hurried. That closer rhythm gave me the impression of a chase after something that was running away: every time the woman was left behind, she tried to catch up with the group—that group which stood for life. I was to recognize her in the course of the night by that peculiar clog of hers—a corpse on the side of the road.

"We, too, expected to be evacuated any moment. And soon, the order came. We pillaged everything, trying to take blankets and anything else that might protect us from the cold. I took two military blankets, and put on two pairs of foot cloths; a doctor friend gave me a shirt and a pair of underpants; we managed to obtain a loaf of bread. We were ready to leave. My friend persuaded me to put the blankets and bread in an infirmary cart carrying medical supplies. It seemed a good idea because the blankets were heavy and we were expecting the trip to be very long.

"There were two thousand of us. I lined up with the doctor in the so-called sanitary department. We were hoping to receive special treatment. As a matter of fact, the SS had a very special treatment reserved for us: in a hayloft, they killed 250 prisoners who were run-down and could no longer walk, by machine-gun fire.

"We were leaving in groups of four hundred. It happened that the doctor and I were included in the group immediately preceding the infirmary one, which was given a completely different itinerary. At seven in the evening, we left the camp where we had suffered so much, but we left it regretfully, certain that we were going towards an even worse fate. I would have preferred to stay, and go back to working at the pit of the mine, instead of witnessing in just a few days what I will now attempt to describe.

"It was a Thursday, and already dark when we left. The intense cold congealed us, and some who seemed to be in the know declared that the thermometer had probably fallen to twenty-five degrees centigrade below zero. The icy road ran straight through a boundless plain. Houses, and groups of houses, broke this monotony. The SS with their dogs flanked the column of prisoners. For every two hundred men, there were ten SS, aside from the ones who patrolled us from one end of the column to the other, on motorcycle or on horseback. During the first hours of the march, we were practically made to run, so that we would not have the strength to escape. I think it was an unnecessary precaution because we were already exhausted when we set out. Towards midnight, the dogs' barking and the shouts of the SS subsided. We could walk slowly, think a little. Thought is a delight, especially in times of misfortune: transporting us to other places and circumstances, it renders us impervious to all.

"We put one foot in front of the other, nostalgically thinking of the places we were leaving, which the Russians would in all likelihood occupy. The imagination was given free rein: some said that the Russians were at our heels, that armed forces had overtaken us on the left; the more optimistic speculated on hypothetical launches of parachutists, sent expressly to rescue us. We believed everything, taking everything for sound currency, but in our heart of hearts there was something bitter, something instinctive; something that was the truth. It was strewn by the roadside: we saw dozens of women who had been killed and abandoned, lying in the oddest positions. One could tell they were young from the shape of their bodies, but their faces were aged by suffering. This was reality; it was what awaited us on the morrow if we could no longer walk.

"We marched till morning, when we headed toward an old ruined house which we could barely make out in the first glimmers of dawn. We were amassed together, all two thousand of us. The SS ordered us to sit, firing their pistols to intimidate us, and shouting. It was impossible to bend, crammed as we were. Many were suffocating. I found myself in a strange position, with my legs bent, pressed on all sides, my feet frozen on the ice, and my forehead frozen by a northern wind. But we could have borne the wind: every now and then a bullet whistled above our heads. The SS were afraid that someone would get up and run away, so they randomly fired shots in the air. I remained in that unbalanced position for four hours. I could no longer feel my legs, which were cramped and numb from the cold. When dawn came we were allowed to stretch our legs a little. I worried that there was no sign of the infirmary group. We had neither the bread nor the blankets we had salvaged. With the doctor, a young man from Salonika, I scrounged two microscopic slices of bread. We hadn't eaten in twenty hours, though we had supplied an effort far beyond our strength.

"When we resumed the march, I saw someone being killed for the first time. We had lined up, and two prisoners, in spite of orders, remained on the ground. When the head of the SS commanded them to walk, one of them sat up, and extended his arms in supplication. The commander nodded to two SS, who carried the two men a few hundred meters away: two shots, two holes in the neck, two corpses. They were the first in a long line. We started to walk, feeling more tired than when we had stopped. We thought of the blankets—to spend another night in the cold without adequate cover would mean certain death. We eyed the blanket of a dead man, and that of another, and took them. That much was taken care of. But unfortunately we were at the rear of the column; two hundred meters from us, the command führer and his adjutant were ready to fire on anyone who halted. Two more had remained on the ground; another struggled. He begged me to help him: I let him lean on me, dragged him a few kilometers, but soon couldn't bear to anymore; I felt him become heavier and heavier, and my own strength ebbed; I felt the pangs of conscience at the idea of leaving him—he faced certain death, but if I took him along, we might both live awhile longer, then ultimately face the same end.

"I was in that dilemma when the trailer of one of the commanders went by. The latter was an Aryan who had strangled his wife and was happily serving his prison term in concentration camp. As an Aryan commander, he had the right to a trailer. With all my courage I turned to him. I don't know what did it, perhaps it was the prisoner's extreme emaciation, but he agreed to take him on. As soon as I was free of my charge, I walked quickly with my friend to rejoin the head of the column. I didn't want to confront a similar situation again.

"Midday had come and gone and our hunger grew; we ate a little bit of snow, but it didn't help. My friend decided to go off in search of a cook he knew. From that moment, I lost sight of him, only to find him some time later at Buchenwald, reduced to a piteous state. It was evening, and still we walked. The cold grew more intense, and for over twenty-four hours we hadn't drunk anything hot. We walked without knowing where we went, when we would stop, or for how many more days we would have to continue our march. We were at the end of our resources, when suddenly the rumor spread that we would be loaded onto a train at a nearby station. We breathed a sigh of relief, but there was no station in sight. Nearby, on the left, we saw flares of light, followed by heavy artillery fire; I was partly glad that our oppressors suffered, too, but worried because the railroad tracks were being bombed, which meant that we might have to continue on foot. I couldn't bear it any more. I closed my eyes and continued to walk slowly, dragging my feet. I walked and every now and then muffled pistol shots were heard, and every time it was the sound of hopes dying, of sufferings and torments ended. I walked and within me an uninterrupted sequence of images unrolled. I walked realizing that my strength was dwindling, as others overtook me. I fell behind, and greeted death. No regrets, no chagrin: I left many who would go on thinking of me. (I believe that our lives continue as long as there is someone to remember us.) I felt nostalgia for my twenty-seven years of age, a simple nostalgia without rebellion; death is not so frightening when one has become accustomed to the idea of dying. One does not suffer, but rather anxiously awaits its arrival. In the end, life is nothing but a set of habits.

"It was deepest night and still we walked. I had reached the limit of my strength, I felt I could not go on, and at the same time no longer felt tired; my legs dragged a body that grew increasingly heavy, while my mind, completely detached from it, precipitously relived the past. It was a strange sweet sensation to relive my life in a sequence of vivid images, as a spectator. All inhibitions were let loose. The word 'train' took me out of that reverie and back to reality. In one second, the strength which I had felt ebbing a moment earlier returned: I pressed forward. But we still had long to wait. We entered the station by turns. I couldn't bear to wait on my feet, in the cold, for several hours. I therefore devised a stratagem that, as luck would have it, worked: among the prisoners, I sought out the three or four who were the worst off, but in spite of everything still held up. I dragged them with me and went up to the SS saying that I was a doctor and that I had been assigned to lead those men to the infirmary wagon. The SS made inquiries among the other prisoners and having confirmed my statement, let me pass.

"It was some infirmary: if only there had been the usual covered cattle wagons—here we found open wagons, with a two-inch layer of snow mixed with coal pebbles at the bottom. We didn't look too closely and threw ourselves into the first empty wagon. I wrapped myself up completely in my blanket and fell asleep. I recall being forced to defend my blanket in the course of the night, kicking the intruders, and being whipped several times, though I didn't pay much attention to it at the time. When I got up the next day, I was drenched. The heat of my body had melted the snow, and the moisture had penetrated through to my bones. I started shivering from the cold, and the next day I was struck with a classic case of acute articular rheumatism, with a temperature of thirty-eight or thirty-nine degrees centigrade: my knees and ankles were swelling and becoming increasingly painful. Every now and then, it snowed, and I pulled my wet blanket over my head. The wagon had filled up, there were about fifty of us, one on top of the other, crowded into two-thirds of the space, as one-third had been appropriated by two *Blockältesters* and their minions, who had fought us off with a whip and now lay in two comfortable beds with blankets and duvets. There was no question of trespassing on their space. The minions were even fiercer than their superiors in meting out retribution. (Since the *Blockältesters* were prisoners serving sentences and could not go to brothels, they were given young boys, aged twelve, sometimes younger, who would in this way be saved from the ovens.)

"By giving cigarettes to the SS on duty, these chiefs were able to obtain a stake and some coal with which, for the duration of the trip, they roasted half a pig they had stolen from God knows where. Our only taste of it was the aroma that wafted towards us. On the second day, we were given four hundred grams of bread. I ate listlessly, having the strength neither to chew nor to swallow. And our appetite could not have been tickled by what went on around us. A dead prisoner had been placed face down in a corner, and there he remained throughout the trip. A Frenchman who had tried to escape was so violently beaten he had gone mad. He lay stretched out all day long and since he had been given an entire package of margarine which he swallowed in a gulp, he came down with a formidable case of dysentery. The stench was unbearable. My knees were so painful and my ankles so swollen I could not move. The wet clothes stuck to my feverish body.

"We traveled in these conditions for two days and three nights. On the morning of the third day we pulled into a small station: it was Weimar, ten kilometers from Buchenwald. The passersby looked at us indifferently, as though they found such a spectacle normal; our wretched state, our drenched clothes seemed to stir no feelings in them. They looked at us coldly, as though to say we deserved all that befell us. Only one young worker in charge of the train's boilers took pity and, escaping the surveillance of the SS, brought us a few liters of hot water, with traces of oil in it. We fell upon that dirty water with avidity and pleasure, regretting only that we couldn't have more of it. From the Weimar station, we saw a wooded hill, at the summit of which rose Buchenwald.

"The surrounding inhabitants had named this the 'hill of blood,' but they did not take the slightest interest in what went on there, since they were persuaded that its inmates must be the greatest enemies of the Reich. Through magnificent woods, slowly, very slowly, the train finally reached Buchenwald. It had a more somber and lugubrious aspect than Auschwitz. There were fifteen-meter-high surveillance towers all around it and beyond the wire fences, at one-hundred-meter intervals. The woods stopped about five hundred meters from the camp, leaving a vast empty space. The entrance was made of reinforced concrete, with an imposing set of iron bars. Above it, if I remember correctly, was the very visible inscription 'Recht Unrecht das ist mein Vaterland das ist mein Recht' (Right or wrong, this is my fatherland, this is my right). Immediately past the entrance there was a great 'piazza,' called Appel Platz, which could accommodate more than forty thousand people. This was where we had to assemble, morning and night, to be counted. But the most meticulous, tedious, and painstaking count was the evening one. When we returned, tired after twelve hours of work, we had to line up, block by block, and march to the square. No one could stay in the blocks. Those who had the misfortune of dying after midday had to be carried to the Appel Platz to be counted, as each block's statistics had to be delivered every day at midday precisely. And so one saw corpses stretched out on two planks, or sitting up on some derelict stool, head and limbs moving eerily to the gait of those carrying them. The corpses were placed beside each block's group, and the SS blithely counted them as they went by. We did not pity the dead much, they were past suffering. But the invalids who had not been accepted into the infirmary, who were in pain and feverish, were also subjected to this torment every night. Several times, I accompanied a man suffering from an undiagnosed pneumonia. At the square, we remained standing for at least one hour and a half if everything went well, but if the numbers did not add up we waited four, even five hours without interruption. The SS, wrapped in ample capes, kept warm in their towers, while we remained outside, in the rain, snow, and freezing weather, collapsing with fatigue, our teeth chattering. (Not infrequently, when we returned, having no change of clothes, we slept naked so as to allow our clothes to dry.) While we stood and waited, our eyes followed the little path that led to the cremation oven; its chimney was always lit by red flames surmounted by a plume of blackest smoke.

"After the arrival of the Americans I was able to visit the construction that had stirred such fear and repulsion in us. It consisted of two floors, a ground level and an underground one. The former contained the cremation oven, with three compartments so that three corpses could be burned simultaneously. When I visited it, there were still some charred remains of skulls and rib cages. That oven was used for those who died 'normally,' while those who were to be eliminated were sent to Auschwitz. When Auschwitz was occupied by the Russians, the unfit were apparently eliminated by intravenous injections of gasoline. It is a fact that anyone in their right mind tried to avoid any kind of injection. The ashes of the German Aryans were collected into urns which were sent to their families. The ashes of all others, whatever their nationality, were scattered. The corpses were piled up in a little courtyard next to the oven, but towards the end the oven no longer managed to consume all that material. Every day, two hundred prisoners died of natural causes. Were you expecting a much larger figure? Let me give you an example. In Rome, which has a population of a million and a half inhabitants, about sixty or seventy people die each day. For a population of forty thousand prisoners, two hundred dead a day is a considerable number.

"In the last two months, the cremation oven at Buchenwald no longer functioned. At some distance from the camp, large graves about thirty meters in diameter, and quite deep, were dug, but they filled up quickly. After the arrival of the Americans I also saw the list of the dead. Next to each name had been inscribed the diagnosis and cause of death. Out of curiosity, I tried to find the name of a Roman friend who had gone from weighing eighty-five kilos to thirty-six before he died. He, too, was given a perfect diagnosis: heart failure.

"On the underground floor were the torture chambers. They were rather low and dark, joined by a narrow winding corridor. In one of them, I noticed all around the walls forty-eight hooks. The prisoners were hung to these hooks from their wrists, which had first been tied behind their backs. In that position they were left from half an hour to three hours, until they either fainted or confessed from the pain of broken bones and sprains. Those tortured were for the most part political prisoners who were lifted from the camp and subjected for various days to the most rigorous and cruel questioning. In a contiguous room stood a gallows and three sliding knots. There, the tortured prisoners who could not yield any more information were finished off. There was also a table onto which prisoners were tied, and the punishment, according to the crime, consisted of a variable number of blows delivered with a knotted cane. Two SS wearing a long white smock with their initials and rank embroidered on the left side of the chest, armed with a long whip, had all the punishments and tortures executed by prisoners who had been especially selected for the task; they themselves didn't lift a finger. In these rooms, after forty-eight hours of continuous torture, the camp commander of Buchenwald, an anti-Nazi German prisoner, went to his death for refusing to reveal to the SS the names of members of the camp's secret organization.

"Buchenwald, unlike Auschwitz, was ruled by political prisoners who wore a red triangle on their chest with the point facing down, and next to it a registration number; the common prisoners, who were fewer and wore green triangles, had been removed from the higher posts, especially the command posts, although the SS still made use of them for certain especially cruel tasks. There were relatively few Jews, twelve thousand, who were confined to four blocks and could not mix with the others. They wore two juxtaposed triangles, a red one pointing up and a yellow one pointing down. The political prisoners, especially those of left-wing parties, had managed to create an internal secret organization which was to save the camp from complete evacuation before the arrival of the Americans. Within the camp, there was also a proper police force made up of prisoners, who answered to the camp commander, assisted by two counselors. The commander, in turn, took orders directly from the SS, and was in charge of seeing that they were carried out. When a specific number of prisoners was needed to go and work in the camps around Buchenwald, the SS transmitted the order to the camp commander, who was free to choose whoever he wanted for the task, as long as the required number was met. So prisoners who had no political affiliations were dispatched to the smaller camps, which were much worse than Buchenwald, while those who were politically active were held back, and if possible, helped.

"At some distance from the cremation oven rose another building, even more horrid and sinister. There, the doctors of the SS performed strange experiments. Vivisection was the order of the day. They tried, by boiling human limbs, to extract from the muscles a substance that could be injected to restore energy. They sacrificed a great many people in an attempt to prove the effectiveness of a new serum against typhoid fever, but without conclusive results. The victims were inoculated with the serum after previously having been infected with typhus germs.

"Aside from the cremation oven and the experiments building, there was another site of torture and terror: it was the so-called small camp. It was within the large one, but divided from it by a series of fences, and by about fifty prisoner policemen, who made sure that no one from the small camp went to the large one. When the SS wanted to punish someone for a grave misdeed, they transferred him to the small camp. That was where we were taken when we arrived. But first we had to go through the usual procedures of shaving, disinfection, and distribution of uniforms. Almost twenty hours after our arrival, spent on our feet, we were led to a block in the small camp. There, we found a prisoner in charge of teaching us how to sleep—two to a bunk, lying on one side, one's head next to the other's feet, so that it was impossible to make even the smallest movement during the night.

"Those who couldn't work, and new arrivals, were put into the small camp. Because Buchenwald was near the center of Germany, all evacuated prisoners were sent there, so that in blocks that had normally housed three hundred individuals, there were fifteen hundred prisoners, sometimes more. The first night, on account of the fever and discomfort, I was unable to sleep. But on the following nights, exhaustion or habit must have prevailed because I slept better than ever. The worst part was when the person sleeping next to us died: we had to keep him there for two or three days, since the block chiefs continued to report him as living so as to collect his ration. Once certified, the dead would be stored in a little room at the entrance to the block, and from there every morning a cart would take the corpses and pile them in a courtyard next to the cremation oven.

"We were awakened at dawn, usually beaten out of sleep, to

be served a coffee that contained everything except coffee. I would have preferred to be left in peace. Immediately after, we were made to go outdoors for the remainder of the day. At first, all we did was run up and down to keep warm; but later, we found it wiser, in order to spare our forces, to huddle tight against one another in groups of one to two hundred. There was a Hungarian Jew, all shrunken, his face twisted with the cold, who fell lifeless to the ground. Two charitable Frenchmen hoisted him to his feet, but the Hungarian fell again. Again, the Frenchmen lifted him up. This happened three or four times. Finally, in a fit of nervous laughter, I told them I thought it would be more humane to let him die lying down rather than standing up. And so it was: five minutes later the poor man's face became serene.

"Every three days, the garbage was collected and taken out of the camp on a big cart. It carried all manner of refuse, potato peel and rotting turnips, and gave off a fetid, nauseating stench. The cart was always followed by a procession of starving prisoners ready to pounce on it the moment something distracted its brutal driver, who was armed with a long whip. I don't know what those potato skins and rotten turnips tasted like, but the fact is that they were consumed with great avidity and gusto. The consequences were seen some time later, when dysentery took its toll. Just to be in the dysentery quarters of the infirmary was sufficient cause of death. It was impossible to keep them clean, given the nature of the disease. The other sections of the infirmary were well maintained but there were hardly any ailing Jews in them: they were either kept in the small camp or sent to some of the other camps around Buchenwald, where death was certain to liberate them soon. On three

142

occasions, I was selected to be on one of those convoys, from which I would not have made it back alive. But all three times, some French friends I had advised and treated saved me, using their political influence on my behalf. Later they even managed to have me transferred to the large camp, and thanks to my name, have me assigned to a block of Russian Aryans, where I passed myself off as a Frenchman of Russian descent. This undoubtedly proved to be my salvation, as from that moment on, I was no longer harassed for anything regarding the question of race.

"All the same, there was no lack of work. I was assigned to a stone quarry; the stones had to be carried up a steep incline and piled onto a wagon that was dragged by fifteen prisoners, each tied to a rope. A supervisor with a long whip followed us closely, reminding us to keep the rope taut. Pulling the wagon smacked to me of slavery, which demoralized me; so I opted for extracting stones, though a more strenuous task. The quarry was dug out of argil soil, which because of the snow and rain was always full of puddles and mud. I sank into it up to my ankles, and since on account of the swelling from the rheumatism my shoes were very large, at every step my feet emerged unshod; finally I decided to work barefoot, so as not to incur the wrath of the SS.

"Barefoot, muddied, my clothes drenched and torn so my skin was exposed, bearing a heavy muddy stone in my arms, walking laboriously, with the threat of the SS behind me, I thought of how wonderful it would be to live free, to find joy in trifles. Life goes by and we never consider ourselves entirely happy, as we struggle under one or another burden. There, in the stone quarry, isolated from the world for a year and a half, life tainted by our idealistic hopes appeared to us very different from what it actually is. We bore all suffering and pain in the anxious expectation of one day regaining our freedom.

"One morning, I was awakened at about three-thirty and told to go to the Appel Platz immediately. Not knowing why, or where I would be taken, still half asleep, I got up hastily, ate half a ration, saving the other half for a time of greater hunger. On the Appel Platz, I found another sixty prisoners, who also had no idea where they were being taken. We were loaded onto a cattle wagon, so crowded we could not move, and driven to the small station at Weimar. There, we lined up and were flanked by ten SS and their police dogs. We walked along a country road, full of puddles and mud on account of the melting snow. If we tried to sidestep the puddles for firmer ground, even before we were hit by the guard's rifle butt, we were bitten in the calves by the dogs. Those dogs were trained to attack dummies dressed like us. After a few disastrous attempts, it became preferable to keep strictly in line, though our shoes filled with water and mud.

"We followed that road for a few kilometers, and emerged into the open countryside. The sun had not yet risen but the hazy brightness that is a harbinger of dawn further blurred our vision. I saw a large ditch in the distance. I thought, then, that in such a deserted plain it would have been easy to shoot and bury us without anyone knowing. In the camp, we had heard rumors that there were too many of us. I was only sorry to have suffered and borne so much and not have the satisfaction of seeing my family one last time. We approached the ditch, and at the last minute I saw a small shed; anxiety and apprehension gave way to doubt, but when I saw hoes being retrieved from the shed, I was certain that for that day at least, we would be allowed to live. Though drenched and covered in mud, I worked joyously to fill that ditch with earth. And when we were given a half-hour break at midday, I savored my half ration with a pleasure that even the most delectable dishes have failed to elicit in me since. We worked until six, then turned back, down the same road, in the same conditions, arriving at camp in time for roll call. There, we stood for another hour and a half till we were brought some lukewarm soup. On the next day, we awoke again at three-thirty to start another day, identical to the first, with the dogs, the mud, the water, the hunger, sleepiness, exhaustion, fearing that life would have nothing but an infinite number of such days in store for us. Dwelling on that possibility, I thought I would go mad. But hope, even in the most tragic circumstances, lent us new courage: the Allies would arrive. And they did.

"Just when we were so exhausted from work that we began to think all our efforts at survival had been in vain, we were given the order that no one was to leave camp for any reason whatsoever. Suddenly, we were in a state of alarm: to stay at the camp and not work was something that couldn't happen without a serious reason. Meanwhile the small camp was filling up with prisoners evacuated from the eastern camps. The secret committee ordered us to stop appearing for roll call. (It was a very intelligent order, as we were to understand later when we found out that, seventy kilometers from Buchenwald, in another small camp, eighteen hundred prisoners had been machine-gunned to death on the Appel Platz.) The SS then requested forty hostages, designated from the most representative prisoners, but did not obtain them: those prisoners were hidden under mattresses, in the lavatories, in hiding places that only the prisoners knew of."

"The SS themselves came to the camp, and the first blocks to be evacuated were those of the Jews. Of the twelve thousand, no more than three thousand reached Dachau. Every day at ten, the alarm sounded, and each of us withdrew into a block with his friends, awaiting fate. Our life was played like a lottery. The SS came down to the camp, a pistol in one hand, a stick in the other, and no sound was heard aside from their sinister steps. We waited anxiously, and when the choice had fallen on another block, we selfishly heaved a sigh of relief. It was by passive resistance that we could win: we had to remain in the camp as long as possible. There were not many SS, whereas there were by then sixty thousand of us. They were trying to evacuate us gradually—about eight thousand men a day. I sided with the French, and for the second time, they saved me; I went with them to block number thirty-four, whereas mine, number forty-four, was evacuated on the second day. The SS wanted to concentrate all the prisoners in Bavaria, in the Tyrol, and in the Alps, where they hoped to offer resistance until such time as armed with new weapons they would be able to take their revenge. But very few of the prisoners reached their intended destination.

"We remained thus five days and five nights, between life and death, hardly eating or sleeping, while we heard the roar of cannon fire at the end of the valley. My heart was heavy at the thought of leaving, now that we were so near to being liberated. One evening, we saw a plane fly over the camp several times. The next day, at about one in the afternoon, we heard, close by, the crackling of machine-gun fire. We found out later that if the Americans had delayed by even a few hours, a specialized

SS detail had devised a diabolically ingenious plan to destroy Buchenwald: they would set fire to the blocks, place heavy machine guns outside the fences, in which they would have opened breaches through which we would pass to escape from the fire: that way we would be legally killed in the act of attempting to escape. But it was the American tanks, by specific order of their commander, who took the camp by storm, while the SS hid in the woods, and took off the uniforms they had once worn with such pride, now become so heavy; we later found shreds of those uniforms hastily cast off here and there.

"The Americans went by, standing upright in their tanks, simply saluting with their index and middle fingers raised in the sign of victory, while with the other hand they distributed cigarettes and canned food. They were covered in dirt, and dusty, but smiled at us. When we asked them to stop, they conveyed that they were in a hurry. But I kept in my eyes and in my heart the white star I had seen through the bars of my prison cell in Rome, when the Allies were still only at Anzio and day after day we had waited for them. A new star rose, bringing hope, perhaps peace and well-being, to this old world racked by insane passions. We watched unconscious and disbelieving, and those eyes of ours which had remained dry in the face of death now suddenly wept in the face of life. Illusion, and life, returned.

"I survived because I took the situation day by day. I knew that my whole family was safe in Egypt—and that helped. When I left the camps, I weighed forty or forty-five kilos. In Rome I got my strength back. When I got off a freight ship in Port Said, I ate ten bananas in a row."

V

In 1940 my grandfather Silvio was arrested for being a "dangerous fascist" because he was president of the Benito Mussolini Italian Hospital in Alexandria, though the problem was not only a semantic one. He had been a solid fascist until the racial laws were passed; Mussolini had not been against Jews until he threw in his lot, and Italy's, with Hitler's. Mussolini declared war on France and England, and on the same evening of his famous speech from the balcony of Palazzo Venezia, my grandfather was interned for twenty-seven days in what had been a lazaret for contagious diseases with other Italians, among them my other grandfather, his daughter's future father-in-law. Wives took turns bringing them feasts from home every day.

It was torrid, he took two showers a day, and passed the time playing bocce, ping-pong, and pining. One night, he was awakened by the sound of bombs. He opened the window and saw a wondrous moon and the spectacle of Alexandria being bombarded. Unable to sleep, his imperturbable roommate Bianchi picked up the insecticide pump and hunted down mosquitoes.

Neapolitan jokes and Neapolitan songs, some cases of colitis. A second camp that had a tennis court with no balls, and a swimming pool with no water, then freedom. In the end he was grateful to Mussolini for passing the racial laws, as the English were lenient towards Italian Jews, Dodecanesians and Libyans.

But the war continued. At the house in Alexandria, an underground bomb shelter had been built, at my grandmother's insistence, and when the siren sounded, all would dive below ground, though my mother and uncles had to be torn first from their beds, then from the wonder of bombs exploding "like little red balloons in the sky," and the sight of approaching Italian and German aircraft. During the Suez Canal crisis, in '56, my brothers and I slept in that very shelter at night, grateful for the novelty of it. One bomb exploded in the garden, wounding a servant, and killing another; all that was left of him was a crater in the ground, a pool of blood, a red fez.

My mother was in her teens and attending the English Girls' School in Alexandria. War provided an unreal, somewhat menacing backdrop to more interesting things: she danced on the terrace by the pool of the Sporting Club to the music of a portable gramophone, played tennis, went to the beach and to the cinema. Only sugar was rationed, and aside from curfew and all the English, Australian, and Indian military personnel in town (later, Polish, French, and American, too), war was elsewhere.

When the front reached El Alamein, fifteen kilometers from Alexandria, there was panic in the city. The family fled to the comfort of Shepherd's Hotel in Cairo and found themselves surrounded by friends and acquaintances who had done the same. There were excursions to the Pyramids, and to Groppi's for ice cream, dancing beneath palm trees and crimson bursts of bougainvillea in the garden of the hotel. The Germans' advance had been checked. The pampered refugees returned to Alexandria and had a quiet summer till the battle of El Alamein.

When the Allies landed in Sicily, there was great euphoria—it seemed the war would end any day. Occasional news from Europe told of arrests, deportations, prisoners of war. My mother said she would have preferred no news and so the illusion that all was well. When she finished school there was no question of her going to university, because there were none in Egypt, because she was a woman, and because of the war. But "occupations" were found for her: drawing, cooking, sewing. She was happy not to have to study any more, she had a boyfriend and, in her words, "life continued carefree and pleasant."

On my way back from Egypt in February 1993, I stopped in Varese for one night. My uncle Piero encouraged me to look through a little chest of drawers stuffed with papers belonging to my grandfather. I asked to take his memoirs with me, and a book titled *La Renaissance d'Egypte*, published by the Egyptian Chamber of Commerce in 1940. It breezes through a few centuries of Alexandria's history:

"Founded by Alexander the Great in 332 B.C., embellished by the Ptolemies, this center of Hellenic genius shone brilliantly for over three centuries as the unrivaled metropolis of the world. It came under the rule of Romans, who appointed prefects to Alexandria . . . After the tragic death of Cleopatra, that fearless beauty whom no one could resist, its misfortunes commenced.

"When Bonaparte's army landed there it was but a small borough of 5,000 inhabitants.

"Mohammed Ali raised Alexandria from amidst its ruins, and made it, in less than a century, the commercial capital of the country and one of the principal ports of the Mediterranean.

"Roman patricians, not to mention the Greeks, favored its beaches, which retain their natural beauty and to which are now added the many advantages of modern civilization.

"Night falls with a suddenness characteristic of tropical countries. Little by little on the beaches lamps are lit in every cabin: a makeshift table is set and one partakes of meals with double the usual appetite owing to the pureness of the sea air. A few gramophones or portable wireless sets diffuse the latest dance tunes, and whilst some couples are lulled by the sweet melodies or exalted by the wild 'Rumba,' others indulge in a game of bridge or in an idle reverie beneath the starlit sky. Then the music dies down and the silent slumbering beach is enveloped in the eternal murmur of the waves."

Amid tinted photographs of Pompey's Pillar, "Native Streets," and "Old Temples," I found a sepia one of my grandfather and his two brothers with the caption: "The firm Pinto & Co. is now included among those that rank highest in the export of Egyptian cotton."

Cotton. I saw fields of it, not in Egypt but in Greenville, Mississippi. How could I know it would move me? I was brought to the fields by a little plane precipitating wildly in the heavens, shuddering through gusts of wind, buffeted sideways, and down, then up as though over a sudden peak. I prayed. A column of crawling fear hardened from my throat to the pit of my belly. Next time I would stay home, but this was a gesture to my grandfather Pinto, Commander of Cotton of the Order of the Nile. I wear a cotton T-shirt every day of my life, sleep in one. Cotton. In Greenville, leaving the death of the certainty of sudden death suspended in the stuffy interior of the four-seater Cessna, I walked on uncertain feet towards cotton fields. Dust, dust on leaves, the color of rusted iron, and the four-tipped cloud of a cotton plant, a faint shadow like a smudge on a photograph where the seeds are. I picked a bouquet of different types, the fleece and white of each distinct. Coming all the way, braving the little hell of my cowardice, to see what the commander had seen—fields of cotton, and with the sight of them, the notion of a living.

The German Mr. Reinhardt didn't want to let him see the mills at Minet el Bassal but the pre-commander fingered every sample he was bid to send, learned to tell the difference between Giza and Karnak: his father was a cotton classifier.

Cotton. The house in Bulkley with seven thousand square meters of garden, the arbor, the Moorish dining room with mosaic walls—thanks to cotton. The chalet in Agami by the sea, paths of thatched fallen pine needles on sand and gridded pavements, white sand from the beach, casuarinas waving lace branches, putting up a coy divide between sun and earth, mixing the fragrance of sky with the fragrance of scorched earth, of iodine, and the sight blinded by blinding sun, thanks to cotton.

How he was coopted into the Order of the Nile: "At a cocktail party in Siouf—a lovely house with a splendid garden—I found myself standing at the bar with the host, Della Porta, and with Makram Ebeid, Nahhās's minister of finance, and a Copt. At least one minister had to be Copt while the others

152

could be Moslem, or as Sedky Pasha called them, 'Egyptian Egyptians.' I was president of the Cotton Exchange and had been active introducing a new variety of cotton, the 'Giza 7,' on the stock exchange. Ebeid said to me, 'Mr. Pinto, what are you?' 'I am Italian,' I replied. He said, 'No, I mean what decorations have you received?' I said, 'I am Commander of the Crown of Italy.' 'No, no,' the man insisted, 'what is your Egyptian decoration?' I replied, 'I have none.' 'Ah, very well,' he said. A week later, the governor of Alexandria summoned me, 'You have been named Commander of the Order of the Nile (third degree) and here are the insignias.' 'Thank you very much, Excellency,' I said. And he said, *'Hat el tani,'* meaning, 'Give me the previous decoration.' But I didn't have one because I had been named commander directly. Old insignias were given to someone else to save money."

Making a living and making a fortune. The first is harder to do, a closer link between work and pay—because the essential piece in making a fortune in cotton is the cotton plant itself: there is no manufacturing one. But provided you have the soil, the climate, the water—Egypt and the Nile—as the *Renaissance of Egypt* put it, "This controlled, dammed and disciplined river distributes its water along thousands of kilometers of canals . . ."

The commander had favorable circumstances: geography and climate. And? More favorable circumstances: "The Mohammedan code strictly forbids usury and pious Mohammedans followed the injunction to the strict letter of the law. In Egypt, moneylending passed into the hands of Copts, Jews, and foreigners, thus in finance as in commerce, foreigners found themselves in a privileged position."

My grandmother spent money from cotton on silk with

which to embroider, on chocolate for mousse, emeralds and amethysts for a ring, seeds for a flower bed, sable skins for a stole, pearls and rubies for a handbag clasp on gathered grosgrain like a pursed mouth around three objects for an evening: lipstick, lace handkerchief, gold monogrammed powder compact. He must have spent more than she, aside from the houses and cars, and the servants' wages, and yearly journeys by boat for eight or ten people from Alexandria to Venice and back. Holidays that lasted three months. In Venice, one summer, having gone with Piero to visit an Italian warship moored in front of the Ducal Palace, he fell into the lagoon: "I was wearing a light summer suit, a panama hat, a Leica around my neck. I put my foot a little to the side of the boat and it capsized. I swallowed the putrid water of the lagoon, my panama hat was ruined, my wallet with all the bills in it was as stiff as dried cod. I had to send the camera and my watch to be repaired. Dripping wet, I had to cross the entire hallway of the Danieli to reach the elevator."

He described the contents of the Isotta Fraschini another summer in Montreux: my mother, her three brothers, Miss Lee, the nanny, his wife, her sister Nelly, the driver and himself. "Overtake the train," the children shouted excitedly. The driver obeyed. Just then, a calf crossed the road. The car swerved off to the side in an attempt to avoid it. The nanny was suspended by her blouse, a gash in her head. The commander, scratched and bloodied by a prickly bush, described as "an Italian count" in next day's Lausanne *Gazette,* had to give away some of his cotton money—to reimburse the owner of the calf, the Swiss phone company for the pole they had overturned, the owner of the field into which they had landed. Miss Lee remained at the hospital in Sierre for over a month. The commander said that he "went back to Sierre regularly to visit Miss Lee" until she told him to tell the doctor she would die if she had to spend one more day in that "damned place." According to his diaries, *he went back to Sierre regularly to visit Miss Lee.* Some cotton money went to women. My mother heard her parents' terrible rows behind the closed doors of their bedroom. My father saw a packet of condoms on the silver tray in that very room when he went there after the death of the prodigal son Gino. Cotton money had gone to him, too. Gino, whose silver trophies lined an entire shelf in Varese, wanted a horse for his birthday and the commander had agreed to buy him one, though he lived in constant fear that his son would die falling off one. He would win every jumping competition now, Gino bragged to his friends. But he went to a party, and on the way home in his car he failed to see the farm cart. My grandparents drove from Bulkley to the hospital at Mazarita, and there, at the entrance, the night porter bowed very low and said, "Please be welcome," and they understood that their son had died. Nissim went to the morgue the next day and cut a lock of hair from Gino's head which he gave to my grandmother. At the funeral, Pierre, who had been his friend, recognized the shape of his body through the shroud.

A woman called: she had a date to go to the beach with Gino. He had a reputation for being a philanderer, almost a requirement in that place and time. Mr. Sursock, who was to sell his horse to him, also called. Everyone thought it was envy that had killed Gino after the magnificence of the wedding—my parents' wedding. Cotton money for the grandest feast Alexandria had seen, at the house in Bulkley with more than a thousand guests. There is a photograph of my mother in her wedding dress—another trade of cotton for silk. My father refused to be in the picture. She stood, white lace making a frail triangular parapet on her head, then precipitating to the ground like a beam of light through a crevice. They were at the chalet in Agami, still honeymooning, when news of Gino's death reached them.

In spite of all his cotton money, the commander lived beyond his means, towards the end especially. After his son died, he became convinced that luck had deserted him. But the spending continued along with the dream of Egypt. He could have left, as many expatriates did, without waiting to be impoverished in wealth as well as in status, having to sell his house to settle his debts. Nasser takes most of the blame in the family for the bankruptcy of Pinto Cotton—though there was mismanagement on the part of the family, and profligate spending. To what degree my grandmother knew who was responsible for what is unclear, but officially she designated Nasser the culprit. That is a family tradition, on her side, the ones with the tics and the intermarriages: never to praise any member of the family but also never to believe they could have real faults, a sort of certificate of aboveness—above both failings and achievement because well-born.

The commander didn't believe he could lose Alexandria. He must have kept the knowledge of Egypt's need for independence segregated in an area of his brain. There is evidence that he possessed that knowledge: he was a friend of Nahhās Pasha, head of the Wafd, the Egyptian Nationalist party, which paved the way for Nasser, founded, as he said, by "the great Zaghlūl Pasha," five times prime minister. Nahhās came to Montecatini and could be seen ambling beneath a grey parasol such as the fellahin use, with his formidable wife Zuzu, "a voluptuous and pleasing woman, the kind Middle Eastern men like, and very authoritarian." Nahhās liked to say, *"Ana mish otocràti la democràti, ana taht gezm murati,"* "I am neither an autocrat nor a democrat, I am under my wife's heel." The commander was under his wife's heel, too. He lent his car to Nahhās, who accepted, saying, "I am not as rich as Mr. Bento." But how rich was Mr. Bento? Rich enough to be prodigal: he lent his house in Varese to Mahmoud Khadriya Pasha, to the Princess Khadrina and their court. In return they sent him a gold bracelet set with scarabs; invited him to the palace in Gabares; on hunting expeditions at the pavilion by the lake; to their villa on the banks of the Nile; to the dahabieh moored at Kasr el Dubara, in front of the British residence. That is where he and the family were as Rommel advanced, and where they would have been trapped if the Germans had actually entered Egypt.

"Every one of those houses was fully staffed and the Pasha was often short on cash," ruminated the commander, who must have known what it was like to be short on cash now and then, until at the end of his life, an end which lasted about twenty years, he was constitutionally cashless and had to depend on my father and on his sons for sustenance. He must have known what the Wafd would bring, he couldn't have been for it and not known: an end to Western domination. He seems to have been uncomfortably splayed between the world of many-housed pashas and that of impecunious nationalists. Nahhās himself occasionally lapsed into living the life he managed to corrode at its roots before retiring from political life in 1952. "He was fond of me," the commander reminisced, "because one year, while I was municipal counselor, I uncovered a political plot to oust the only two Egyptian advisers who were members of the Wafd and I resigned, together with some of my European colleagues." Nahhās Pasha knew of this. Any support of the Wafd was in opposition to Farouk. So the commander knew, but he stayed, hoping perhaps for some special immunity from the general course of history in deference to his congeniality. He stayed long enough to see Nasser come to power, and still he stayed, waiting to run through every last cotton cent.

I met him when practically all the life had gone out of him. His sneezes could be heard all over the house and at the bottom of the garden too. They came by the dozen. If he was being pestered, he would put a stop to it by howling piteously, *"Je suis très malade."* His other weapon was deafness. If he didn't want to hear, he would say in the middle of the other's sentence, "What?" and then, at the end, very distinctly, "I didn't hear anything." With the air of one about to impart a mystery, he would recite slowly, "You catch eels when water is up to your heels. You catch bass when water is up to your *mmmm—*" he paused, then concluded triumphantly "—knees."

He loved to eat, collected menus he had been served on ships and at official receptions, but towards the end, his diet dwindled to boiled vegetables. He had been a good-looking man, lost most of his hair by the time he was forty, and by the time he was eighty, a few white strands were carefully combed and brilliantined across his scalp. He wore 4711 cologne, kept a neat moustache, closely clipped, covering his entire lip but only to the edges of the mouth. He wore light blue or white poplin monogrammed shirts, custom-made for him in Alexandria, like most of his clothes, and charcoal grey trousers, flannel in winter and combed wool in the summer, perfectly pressed. His long elegant hands, meticulously manicured, were covered with dark brown spots and a diamond ring graced the little finger of his right hand. His small black eyes were lively, his lower lids puffy—he suffered from weak kidneys and there was always an open bottle of Fiuggi water on a silver tray near him. (Another fortune I have inherited: his stone-producing kidneys.) Sometimes, in the spring, he went to drink the waters at the source.

Judging by his memoirs, what he and his cronies did, for fun, was to gather at watering holes. One year, in Fiuggi, he met Cleopatro Cobianchi, inventor of a profitable chain of underground day hotels. He had been to Egypt as a young man because an Egyptian prince of Turkish origin had taken a shine to his Bolognese girlfriend, a ballerina, and she had agreed to be with him on condition that Cleopatro came, too. The prince had a palace in Cairo, in Kasr el Nil, with an immense garden filled with doves Cleopatro hunted from palm to palm, in the daytime, whereas at night "his pastimes were quite different"; he could still sing the Egyptian pop song *Ta'a lili ya batta, wana mali heh!* ("Come to me, my duckling, why should I resist," or words to that effect).

In his last years, the commander sat in his study, a small room containing a desk he seldom used, "his" armchair, and a little red velvet couch where visitors sat to be scrutinized by him. Of his years in Alexandria, he remembered their comedy, and lack of pining for the past left him room to size up the women who fell into his orbit. I brought a friend from boarding school, and he said, after a thorough inspection of her diminutive, shapely figure, "*Piccola, ma carina.*" On every little table, there were two or more amber Arab rosaries, and ashtrays made of ancient Turkish silver ankle bracelets. On the knob of the door hung a white horse's tail made into a fly swatter that he had used in Egypt. While he spent his mornings reading the paper, writing letters, dictating his memoirs, and later, just sitting, lost in thought, my grandmother was down the hall in her study, embroidering.

If he regretted Egypt and the loss of his fortune he never talked about it, as my grandmother did, missing no opportunity to spit contempt at Nasser. "He should go get blessed," she would say, and it is what my mother says now when Berlusconi appears on television. "Amazing, isn't it?" My brother Giampi said. "She has become a pinko-radical, a commie, really."

My grandfather developed a sort of flirtation with his nurse, especially after my grandmother's sudden death, at dawn one day, of an embolism.

"In 1923 I became engaged to Berthe Tilche," my grandfather wrote in his memoirs, "I was married on March 23rd of that same year. My wife belonged to a distinguished family in financial decline. To say all the good about her would be impossible in these brief notes . . . " So it is that my grandfather dismisses the subject of his marriage.

On the boat from Alexandria to Genoa, it must have been in the twenties, on their honeymoon, my grandmother inquired of her husband whether it was true that children came out of knees. If that was what she knew of sex, then her sister Nelly

160

had the advantage, because she said, "A woman's breasts need only be big enough to fill the hands of an honest man."

Nelly spoke very good French, for an Italian, and very bad Italian, because she had been raised in Switzerland. To her father she owed certain Tuscanisms. Like my grandmother Berthe, she spoke quite fluent Arabic.

When Berthe died and it was suggested to my grandfather that Nelly, who had been living with us in England, could stay with him in Varese, he whispered to my father, "Now that the flesh is gone they want to give me the bone."

How two women of the Mediterranean became so detached from the calls of the flesh is a wonder of the capacity for metamorphosis, and the effects of over-"civilization," or education, as it is known. Which shows that genes set the stage only so that a series of accidents can ruffle the plan.

One, Berthe, embroidered furiously, while the other, Nelly Clementine, anointed herself comptroller of our underwear, and spokesman for the underwear itself, her very special cause being "the disappeared." Our laundry, like anybody else's laundry, had a way of gobbling up a pair of panties here, an undershirt there. From the time that my eldest brother Giampi began to write "Suzy, Suzy, Suzy" all along the sole of his basketball sneakers, Nelly began to notice the disappearance of a certain number of *caleçons*, underpants, from his closets. This fact became the subject of Nelly's morning conferences with my mother.

In Tokyo, my mother would normally return to bed for an hour or so, after having had breakfast with my father and having seen the white-gloved hand of Kikuchi-san, the driver, ceremoniously slam the door of the car on him, and the black Nissan recede down the driveway, coasting the lily pond. Nelly,

161

who was longing for conversation, would not dare interrupt this morning crossword puzzle session, unless there was a serious reason, such as the disappearance of the *caleçon*.

In the end, Nelly, having received an "I don't know, do as you like . . ." from my mother bent on returning to her hour's recreation, would take the matter to my brother and like a pusillanimous cross-examiner, ask every possible question that might push a culprit's back to the wall to unearth the missing link. This ended invariably with Nelly's "Can you call your friend and ask whether you left it there?" followed by Giampi's violent "No!"

How had a woman whose bookshelves were lined with read and reread original editions of Corneille, Molière, Racine, become so enveloped in the life and travels of intimate apparel? Nelly mended socks and underwear. She took on these punishingly tedious tasks so as to justify her existence in our household, just as she could be relied on to say, *"Un tout petit peu,"* just a tiny bit more, whenever she agreed to a second helping. And yet she was a Tilche, one of the venerated families of Alexandria, who had private pavilions at the Jewish cemetery housing their dead, whereas others had to be lined up next to strangers, beneath marble slabs and exposed to the elements. No, it is clear—she fell into the hands of tyrants: her own mother, first and foremost, who found in her, at last, a well-mannered maid and a congenial companion. Her sister, second, who under the guise of taking her in cast her once again in the role of the servant, to be trusted above and beyond the most trusted servant where her four children were concerned. Then us: my parents, my brothers, myself, though I was in league with her, secretly. I was allowed in her room, could borrow books from the library that she had carried from France to Egypt to Italy to Japan.

On top of her bookcase, there were two objects—an ethereal green bowl, the size of a tangerine, with faint white veins running through it, and a miniature urn of milky Lalique glass with chestnut brown flowers climbing up to the narrower mouth. It rested on a wooden base.

In Japan, Nelly broke her leg. I was enlisted to help her wash and, especially, to cut the toenails on the semi-encased foot. The tip of it had to be dipped in very hot water. It was a ritual lasting over an hour, during which I sat patiently, performed my task, and tried to conceal my repulsion at the smell of steam redolent of soaked toes that wafted into my nostrils as the softened nails crumbled off the blade of my scissors.

Nelly's Swiss schooling had addicted her to rather punitive systems of hygiene. Vigor constituted the core of any "treatment" she accorded herself, like a massage of the scalp with a lotion that never seemed to make any difference to her hair (except that it might all have dropped out without it) and left her looking like the madwoman of Chaillot, which was our other nickname for her besides Ben-Gurion. Her morning was spent in this dutiful state of disarray—a sort of counter-vanity.

She wore the same clothes all her life: a straight skirt to below the knee—grey, blue, or brown—a crewneck sweater (cotton in summer, wool in winter), a cardigan. Never any frills, trims or decorations. Just a few pieces of jewelry: a gold chain bracelet with little diamonds and glassy emeralds, and another of little flowers, with pearls on each petal and at the center.

This one had belonged to her mother and can be seen in a photograph of her wearing a long black beaded dress, and her hair puffed and rolled up.

She had Asian skin, Nelly: the Turk in her—firm and yellow, with many raspberry moles. She had no waist, or at least so it seemed, encased as she was all day long in an elastic and bone corset that went from above her waist to just above her knees. This unsexing was adopted by my grandmother, too—a sort of canned silhouette—all reduced to one cylinder, two legs, two arms, head, neck, cropped hair flattened beneath a hair net whose thin elastic was always visible at the hairline and left a dent on the brow. Nelly's legs were short and muscular as a man's. Her arms were sinewy and hairless and her fingers deformed by arthritic bouts that had pushed each of her fingers into new positions—up, down, and sideways—as though to accommodate the new width of the joints. She used them like spatulas, as though the fingers were webbed. When she patted her hair, she flattened it; when she powdered her face with an ostrich puff, thoroughly and matter-of-factly, she left perfect round circles of powder much too pink and much too white for her sallow complexion on her cheeks, chin, eyebrows, eyelashes. The blue eyes twinkled out of a powdery web of lashes. The lipstick came out of a silver container: she pushed a ruby knob up the slot in the tube, and, as she did so, the stick of crimson grease emerged obscenely. The point was always flat at the top: she applied lipstick to her mouth in two straight parallel lines, then rolled her lips in over her teeth so that it would spread, more or less, to the rest of the mouth.

Before going out, she patted her skirt front and back as a final gesture of encouragement for the objects on her to look their best, as if they would have to make do without her. I doubt that she ever looked at herself in the mirror. Yet her eyes were very blue, her hair somewhat, too, because, as she explained, this kept the yellow from showing through. The skill of a hairdresser was judged by his ability to obtain "the right blue." This impalpable tint was one she had in her brain and there is no question that it hovered electrically between periwinkle and lilac, as this was mostly the halo she appeared under after a visit *chez le coiffeur*—a once-a-week proposition. Whatever her notions of beauty, they had very little to do with sex. A woman's décolleté, she thought, was enhanced by *salières*, saltcellars—cavities near the clavicles.

I, too, wear the same clothes every day, like a railway employee. In those days, in Tokyo, I slept in rollers, ironed my hair, slicked it with beer to make it drop down flat, and curled it in a Cleopatra bob. What did I see, in Japan, after all, other than women with lustrous, straight black hair? The girls at my school were not women but girls, like myself, and girls look to women for inspiration. How did my curls fit?

In a shoestore, when I was ten, a Japanese saleslady looked at my feet and said, "*Beh-ry lah-gee*." I had already outgrown their largest size for women, a thirty-seven. My shoes had to be made by a man who specialized in orthopedic shoes, and at his most inspired, the shoes looked like orthopedic shoes with a pretension to elegance. They were always navy blue; the point was reinforced so that after a bit of wear one saw where the support strip had been inserted. Then the top of the shoe burst inexplicably into a series of inlets to the left and right, whose diameter was puckered and drawn together by thin tubular laces. These I tied into stiff cat-whiskers bows.

In Japan Nelly did not have the problem of size. She was barely taller than five feet, though when her hair was made to assume its daily electrocuted erection, she appeared more imposing. She was no taller than most Japanese women. And many members of her family were rather tiny, too, though imperious. The space they occupied, because modest in volume, was not to be violated.

One side of Nelly's family, the Pihas (though others maintain it was the Levys), invaded the space surrounding their anatomy with a flurry of tics. Each member of the family had a different one. Once the family in Alexandria had hired a new waiter—a *sufraghi*. He duly appeared on his first day of employ in the dining room at dinner time, wearing a white belted galabiya and a tall red fez, and bearing a silver platter with the first course. He accosted the first person at the table, who shook one shoulder, a second, who shook her head, a third who winced violently, a fourth who grimaced two or three times, a fifth who shuddered, a sixth who scowled, a seventh who blinked. He took these as signs of the food being declined. He dashed the tray to the ground, swept off his fez and said, "I refuse to work in a house full of mad people!"

Where do the Tilches come from? I look at a photocopy of the family tree drawn by a certain Adrien Piha, in Paris, and dated June 12, 1969 . . . I must ask Pierre who that is. I read the names and feel a wave of nostalgia in place of the usual need to run as far as possible, to be as unlike them as I can. What is this new allegiance? In the names, I read the combination of elements so natural to me and unnatural to most other people—that specific one and another element of religion, race, nationality—that defines me and limits my ability to understand others and their ability to understand me.

The tree has branches, the branches leaves, and the branches, smaller branches. It begins with a certain Elie Behor Levy de Menasce, born in 1759. He married Adèle Aghion. They gave birth to a Yacoub, and under his name the legend reads, "1st baron de Menasce"; how he was made a baron is not known, at least by me. A genealogical tree is frustrating because it doesn't reveal where people were conceived, or how it happened, only the nominal result. This first baron married Esther Naggiar and they gave birth to a Baronne Camille. She married Abramo Piha and had nine children: Elie Bey, Esther, Jacques, Fortunée, Hélène, Mariette, Eugénie, Maurice, and Emilie. From Hélène descended Pierre's branch of the family.

We are direct descendants of Emilie Piha who married Abramino Tilche and had six children: my great-grandmother Gabrielle, and William, Linda, Edouard, Alice, Marie. Of these, three married cousins called Tilche, among them my great-grandmother, who married Marcel Tilche. They had four children, Berthe, Nelly, Georges, Gaston.

My grandmother Berthe, in marrying Silvio Pinto, was marrying beneath her, but in avoiding cousins she gave her descendants a boost. The dates are, at best, approximate. On the page dedicated to Baron Behor de Menasce, one of his sons, Baron Félix, had a daughter Rosette, who had another daughter, Baronne Claire, who married a Vincendon, whose daughter Claude married Lawrence Durrell.

In *The Jews in Modern Egypt, 1914–1952*, by Gudrun Kramer, I find: "The Tilches, another of the presidential families, were one of the very few élite families to be able to trace their presence in Egypt to the sixteenth century. Described as the wealthiest trading house in early nineteenth century Egypt, they had made a fortune in trade with Italy, and, as early as the eighteenth century, moved into banking. Under Muhammad 'Alī they imported gold and silver to embellish military uniforms, engaged in the wheat trade, and then turned increasingly toward cotton growing and ginning . . . ."

Further on: "In the nineteenth and twentieth centuries, Alexandria was generally considered the best organized of all Jewish communities in Egypt." But one man wrote, in 1928: "The Sephardim of Alexandria are entirely under the influence of the French. They imitate the life-style of Parisian high society, leading a totally superficial life, showing no deeper interests, they make a lot of money and spend a lot of money—but have no sense of social work and national responsibility."

Regarding the Pintos: "Italian Jews formed a distinctive group within the so-called Sephardi community. Numbering between 8,000 and 10,000 in the interwar period, they lived mainly in Alexandria . . . Some of the richest and most respected Jewish families in the country, such as the Mosseris, Pintos or Rossis, had Italian nationality."

Among my grandfather's papers, I found a photocopy of a short manuscript entitled "History of the Pinto Family," which begins: "The Pinto family came to Livorno in 1500. In 1800, the Pintos had a factory in Livorno for the production of coral objects. Davide Pinto and his brothers owned it. They also owned many buildings on one street, and there was a saying,

'These houses are not *dipinte,*' painted, 'but di Pinto,' belonging to Pinto. Davide Pinto, an adventurer, embarked on business ventures that ruined him. He was given an allowance based on the real estate he owned. He went first to Tunis with his family, then since one of his daughters was married and living in Egypt, moved there in 1865. Fortunata Pinto married her cousin Alberto Cremisi. He was very intelligent, cultivated, capable of doing anything that went through his head. First he took up mathematics, then he was a carpenter, an ebonist, a pharmacist, a sculptor, embroiderer, and novelist. His time was divided among these manias, and he spent all he earned, which was as much as his brother-in-law Oreste Pinto . . ."

My great-grandfather Oreste had first gone to Egypt in 1863 or 1864 with his parents, who died soon after of cholera, "felled by a cruel morbus," as the inscription on their tomb at the Chatby cemetery reads. At thirteen he went to work, studying at night, to support himself and his three sisters. He grew a stupendous moustache to appear older than his years and was known as Abu Chanab, the man of the great moustache. During the nationalist and military Arabi Pasha revolts, when Europeans were massacred and hung on meat hooks outside the shops on the rue des Soeurs, he borrowed a sack of gold napoleons from an Arab colleague and left for Italy with his family. There were fires and looting till the British landed a month later and after a skirmish with the Red Jackets at Tel al-Kabir defeated Arabi Pasha, and went on to occupy the Cairo Citadel; then repressions were violent and the bodies of Arabs who had been executed were hung on poles adorning the Place des Consuls. My great-grandfather returned to Egypt after being recruited at the Caffè Falchetto in Livorno, where he went every day to read the papers, to be a cotton classifier for the British firm of F. C. Baines & Co.

Almost half a century later, when an Italian minister came to confer on him the Italian knighthood, he told the dignitary, "I came here not quite barefoot but with a pair of shoes that had holes in them. Still, at least I had shoes on."

His wife, according to my grandfather, "was a saintly woman devoted to her children and to the running of her house. She had an iron constitution though she suffered from frequent headaches. At the Pharmacy of Santa Maria Novella in Florence, she always bought a stock of 'anti-hysterical water' and 'vinegar of the seven thieves.' She had seven children and two miscarriages and died at the age of ninety. Every day she read the Italian daily paper, *Messaggero Egiziano*. But when Italy entered the war and it was no longer published, she started reading the French daily, *La Réforme*. She didn't speak French but understood it perfectly. She embroidered to the last days of her life and went out every day at three in the afternoon for a spin in the car. There was an old Berber at the door, and she always gave him a few coins. The man had been servant to a German couple. When war broke out in '39, his employer was interned and he was left alone with the wife. They became lovers, but one day the wife was led away and he went mad with grief. He roamed the streets wailing, '*In alabu el Inglisi,*' 'Damn the English who took her from me!' "

In what used to be my grandfather's desk, in Varese, I found a brown envelope marked in red, "Strange Letters and Oddities." Among them: A check for "00.000 Lira" drawn on the "Bank of

Inflation, Capital: Moscow, signed by the Governor, P. Togliatti," recommending, "Save Italy and your savings."

Letters sent to the social security office in Alexandria that he collected include one from a man who declares, "I live maternally with my concubine"; another from a woman whose husband is "dead for the time being"; a third stating, "Sir, I must inform you that I have been in bed with my doctor for six weeks and that it hasn't had any effect on me."

"Maestro Sebastiano Grasso, Composer, Musician, Artist, Painter," gratefully accepts five Egyptian pounds for his "very modest Triumphant March" which he dedicates to my grandfather's beautiful roses, fortunate enough to inhale his wife's exhalations, and which will one day, he hopes, become big beautiful diamonds ornamenting her lovely waist.

"Your Obadient Servant" writing on "8 OctoBER 1742" informed: "The father of Mohammed wilcome friday to take the food of hen, when you wait in Cairo . . . I like to see all the chief in the room of clothes him in the gardin, he not good & this is a chief man . . ."

"Excellency," complains a wounded sibling, "my fratricides Michel, Anis, Alice and Adèle refuse to live in their lodgings and use robbery to live with me, buy cakes, turkeys, chickens, tins of beef: refusing to leave Egypt like all the other whites . . ."

The guardian, Sayed Ahmad, remonstrates: "It happened that the domestic made a mistake of which I informed la grande Madame Telki [Gabrielle Tilche, my great-grandmother]. The domestic, being cross, gave me orders saying those orders came from you . . ."

Mr. Walter Onofrio complains of unrequited love: "I infinitely regret to have to inform you that Mademoiselle Sylvane

Ladoucette had the cowardly courage to have me ill-treated in Church (the House of God, and a very Holy place) by the individual Egidio Messina in the presence of the Reverend Father Lodovico Toschi and other Priests, till, at one point, said individual, in Church and in treacherous fashion, gave me 4 punches. I regret that a young lady I held in great esteem, should want to *'quereller'* in Church . . . As the Holy Virgin crushed the head of the devil, Saint Teresa of the Child Jesus will crush that of the vain and *mad* Sylvane Ladoucette, an eye for an eye, a tooth for a tooth, she never wanted to understand that one word from me and God will do the rest. If she wants to have peace, all she has to do is marry me, otherwise sooner or later, she will see reason." In a memorandum, with the sign of the cross printed at the top of it, he wonders, "If I who prayed devoutly was sent to an insane asylum, what would happen to a true madman?"

A "Personal and Cofidential" note from a Mademoiselle Hélène Lévy, having learned of the "eleven happy births with which your house has been honored," offers her services as "dry-nurse," in exchange for which she would accept one pound a month, and two days off, during which she would be replaced by her boyfriend.

There are letters expressing gratitude for financial contributions. A newspaper clipping eulogizes, "Silvio Pinto is perhaps the most modest man in Alexandria. He lives by the famous proverb, 'Live hidden to live happy.' Excessively debonair, never violent, his patience is infinite . . . He has a sense of discretion and measure, a perfect mastery of himself and the ease so characteristic of the perfect gentleman that he is."

An invitation from King Farouk, to have tea at the Ras el-Tin Palace, Sunday, July 29, 1945, at 7 P.M.; a card stamped with a golden eagle, "With every good wish for Christmas and the New Year from Gamal Abd El-Nasser." Two Amateur First Prizes from the Alexandria Horticultural Society.

Finally, a tiny envelope addressed to my grandfather and his brother, Ezio, and within it, the even slimmer business card of a "Max De Tawil Bey," Attorney at the Court of Appeals of Alexandria, saying: "Frankly, to tell the truth, properly speaking, if I may be allowed to say, to ask for your young daughter in a marriage of convenience. I apologize, I offer my most sincere thanks. MAX DE TAWIL BEY, The Best Man in the World by His Majesty King George VI, 1938." On the back of the card, there is a list of people from whom "information" should be obtained: "His Eminence, the Rabbi of Alexandria, and that of Cairo, various Pashas, King Farouk, Prince Mohammed Aly and a judge."

The "young daughter" that the Best Man in the World had in mind for a "marriage of convenience" was my mother. She had other plans.

My father was, she said, charming, handsome, very thin. It was a New Year's Eve—December 31, 1943. She was to go out with her brother Aldo and a group of friends. One of them said he would bring a certain Shalom Alhadeff. My mother knew him because they had met in their little English world under the North African sun. That evening, all the men were paired off except for him and another man. My mother told Aldo, "I'll take Shalom, the other's too ugly."

They started going out, secretly; my father didn't want anyone to know because since he was the youngest of seven, his brothers teased him mercilessly. It was hard to avoid them altogether, though; there were so many, my mother said, one was bound to run into at least one or another of them.

They went to the Swiss Chalet, near Stanley Bay, to have English tea. With a degree of pride, she admitted that they had made love before they were married. Where? I asked. Oh, at the Sporting Club. But where at the Sporting Club? Not on a tennis court, surely. There were many bushes, she replied demurely.

"In 1946," my grandfather wrote, "after the end of the war, Nora became engaged to Carlo Alhadeff," he had changed his name by then, "and married him in June." By marrying my mother, though they had a Jewish wedding, my father was already converting, because her family was even less observant than his: they *never* went to temple. They considered themselves Italian and they were assimilated. My father defected, whether he knew it or not, from the island of his family and the island of faith: he, too, wanted to be a European. It was what his father had wanted for his children, and it succeeded.

When France, Britain and Israel declared war against Egypt in 1956, all my grandfather's possessions were blocked and he was included on a list of "rich French Jews of Zionist sentiments." When he remonstrated, the error was rectified and he was moved to a list of "dangerous individuals having Zionist sympathies" and his possessions were confiscated altogether, among them a hunting rifle, a Richard Westley, an ancient panoply, and an axe with a golden inscription in Arabic. The president of Italy intervened and all my grandfather's possessions were restored to him except for the collection of arms.

His memoirs end on a melancholy note:

"While at the start of my career everything came easily, now everything went against the grain. We had bad credits in Egypt—one client alone took more than 25,000 Egyptian pounds from us; there were restrictive laws regarding personnel as the Arabic language became mandatory and we were obliged to hire a surplus of inefficient personnel. We tried to set up commerce in the Sudan, founding Pinto Cotton Sudan Limited . . ."

Often it was fifty degrees centigrade in the shade. The English said of living there, "You don't have to be crazy to live in Khartoum, but it certainly helps." A friend of the family's had accompanied us to the Sudan, where our parents had been living since my grandfather had set up a branch of his company there. They thought we would be safer than in Egypt with the Suez Canal crisis going on, and nightly bomb raids.

There is a picture of my father taken in Khartoum, in which he wears a crimson and black sarong wrapped around his midriff; he was too overweight to be technically good-looking. But he had green eyes, height, the desire to please. The bout of meningitis—one night of intense fever when he was a boy— had left his right leg thinner than his left, and the foot slightly deformed. In a suit, all that emerges is one sleek shoe that points up the exaggerated creases in the other, the foot refusing to rest flat. Women love a hero with a weakness.

When my mother and father separately fell in love with the husband and wife of another couple, she gave up first when she considered that there were three children. She did not feel that this man—black patch over one eye, more athletic than my father—was an alternative.

She says that when my father realized that she had fallen in love, he hastened to withdraw from his affair. Did he still think that it wasn't worth it, exchanging one woman for another, or rather one marriage for another? A friend's father said to him when he announced the breakup of his marriage on account of another woman, "I can understand changing, but for another woman?"

It was so warm in Khartoum we usually slept on wooden beds in the garden. Goats wandered in and out. In the evening, sanitation trucks drawn by camels made the rounds. They were open trucks containing pails of sewage. Most people had outhouses by the edge of the road to make it easier for the sanitation workers to retrieve pails and replace them with empty ones. Once, when my brother Gianchi was using the outhouse, a hand appeared beneath him and performed the switch as he sat there. He ran back to the house hollering in terror.

At a benefit dance in a garden one evening, the raffle prize announced on the loudspeaker was a bottle of eau de cologne. Just then, the shit trucks were going by and the drivers took the mention of eau de cologne as an insult directed at them. They stopped, got out, and overturned the contents of several pails onto the guests.

When the trucks went by, the smell was asphyxiating. The adults were used to it, but we would climb up on the fence and yell insults. We waged war in those days on the German children across the street; we filled jars with mud and jettisoned the contents across the narrow unpaved road onto "the enemy" lined up on the other side. Our friends, Jean-Luc and Guy, joined in.

Their parents and ours had exchanged partners. There is a

photograph taken on the patio in Khartoum: my mother is dancing with J.P., my father with C.P. And that was how it was between them for a time. My parents had been married the proverbial seven years. My father fell in love with the beautiful Chris—the first in a series of women named Chris: that one, then the doctor, and now Cristina. My eldest brother married a Chris, too, though they are now separated. Khartoum Chris had blond hair she wore in a French twist—we called it a banana—was slim, tall, had winking brown eyes, high cheekbones, and a big sexy mouth. They danced to Eartha Kitt's "I'm Just an Old-Fashioned Girl," and to Harry Belafonte's "Matilda."

At first, Pinto Cotton Sudan seemed a success, but then one disastrous year for the cotton harvest surprised the company with irretrievable credits. Another disappointment: they had extended their operations to Kenya; but there too, the crisis in the Congo proved fatal, because they had ordered too many cars and tractors and right then the banks and the credit insurance companies cut their credit off. It was a disaster to be added to those of Egypt and the Sudan. My grandfather sold his villa in Bulkley, which his father had purchased in 1900 for a very small sum, and was never even paid in full for it. With the proceeds, he settled the debts of Pinto Cotton—about sixteen thousand pounds—six days before his departure. On the sixth of June 1960, he and my grandmother left Alexandria with a permit to return but with a one-way ticket only. In Varese, though he had hoped to find at least the crumbs of his fortune, he found only a house to live in which had been their summer house.

An official black and white portrait was taken of Gianchi and me at our school in Azzate. I don't know whether this was to prove to parents that one had indeed been there, or was simply a souvenir in a medium that was then still relatively inaccessible. In the picture my jaw-length hair is flattened back by a headband. I am wearing a black overall, the stiff white plastic collar that was then obligatory in Italian elementary schools, and the white ribbon tied in a bow at the front to hide the button. I look like a rabbit who has sighted danger: my spine is upright, my head slightly tilted to the right, my eyes glinting straight into the camera lens; I sit at my school desk, a map of the world splayed out like a chicken on a spit behind me, my hand holding a plastic pen with the nib poised over a diagonal sheet of paper as if I had been caught in the act of signing a warrant.

Leaving school at lunchtime one day, as we did every day—though we longed to stay and eat the minestrone we had smelled cooking all morning, something we were allowed to do only on rainy days—one of our classmates started yelling, "Livio is dead, Livio is dead." We took up the battle cry and started running across the square. Where we had gotten the idea that seeing a corpse is fun I don't know, except for the fact that everything unknown—such as being an adult—was presumed to be wonderful. Livio was a man in his sixties we sometimes encountered, parked in his wheelchair at the caffè in the piazza, or outside the church. I don't recall ever having talked to him. "Let's go and see Livio," someone shouted. We ran up to a house next to the church. The front door was ajar.

Suddenly quiet, we walked in. In the first room, there were

women in black, sitting on narrow wooden benches around a bare rectangular room, weeping and praying. I went through the door on the right and was seized by terror. I was conscious of the form stretched out under the sheet but could not look beyond his crimson ear and the broken capillaries on his cheek. I stared down at the shoulder resting on the board, at my feet growing out of the mottled marble floor, and was unable to move. Why was death so frightening even before I had had a chance to be prejudiced against it? I could not imagine the "I" being silenced, a time before I could say "I." It felt infinite, something beyond my own flesh and blood. There was no getting away from it. This "I" had seen everything from the beginning of time, and was on loan to me. Without me it would continue, and so I, too, would continue.

That evening, I woke up in the middle of the night, and could feel the presence of the dead man in the room, wheeling himself around. I called to Aunt Nelly in the room next door, desperate for consolation. I wanted to have a breezy conversation, to pretend that my teeth weren't chattering. I was obliged to be much braver then. Now, if I have one of those nights when the room seems animated with ghosts, I think nothing of sleeping with the light on, even the television to watch me in exchange for all the time I have spent watching it over the years. But at the age of seven, I slept in a room by myself and there was no question of keeping the light on.

Nelly came in and turned on the light, which short-circuited like the tail of a firework along the wall. In the dark, she sat on my bed. When I asked if she could see the dead man in the wheelchair, she told me not to be silly, "and things" (she always added that when she was worked up as though to include what she was unable to articulate), and gave me an energetic slap. It did not frighten the dead man away. He would accompany me into adolescence.

The Colossus of San Carlo was so large, the guidebook said, that three people could stand in its nose. But first, one had to reach the pedestal. Nelly was with us. We climbed up a spiral staircase. I padded along the wall with my hands to keep my trembling feet company up the dark winding tunnel. When I reached the platform and went out through a little door to stand on the landing around the feet of the statue, I no longer wanted to go up into its nose. In fact, I wished there were some magic way of instantly being restored to the ground.

I held on to the frail railing and looked down: people walking below looked like moving dots. Shivers of vertigo ran up the back of my legs. My aunt resorted to her favorite method for dealing with psychological situations requiring tact, sensibility, a woman's touch: she said, "That's enough . . . and things," and slapped me. She was right, perhaps, because as the blood flowed back through my limbs after the shock, I was conscious of a desire to get away from her, even if it meant facing the terrible spiral staircase again.

That slap was one of the few things she bragged about for years when it came to discussing our upbringing. She did not say, as any maudlin aunt might have done, "Remember that lovely afternoon at Lake Maggiore . . . ," but rather, "Remember that day at the Colossus of San Carlo . . . when I slapped you . . . and things?"

We caught the measles. The doctor thought he would teach my mother how to administer injections: this he did in front of us. She practiced on a pillow: holding the syringe in her right hand like a pen, as he had shown her, she swiveled her wrist so the needle skewered the pillow. That was all there was to it, he insisted. But later we submitted to her experiments and it became apparent that there is at least one difference between feather down and flesh: the former does not rebel. Elvira the town injectioner was called in, to our relief.

For a time, in the spell of her mission to civilize us, our grandmother was a beast, embroidering and tormenting, forcing us to eat things we disliked, such as beets. My mother couldn't eat them so it was a matter of allegiance to repudiate them. But she was often away in Nairobi with my father, which left my grandmother in charge of our paltry kingdom. The bloody beets, uneaten, would reappear at dinnertime, again at breakfast the next day. I left the dining room in tears and repaired to my room. My eldest brother Giampi would come in, sit by me, and say, very persuasively, "Don't cry, you'll get furrows down your cheeks."

His room was upstairs, above the pantry. He left his fountain pen on the table one day, and when he returned, it was broken. A temporary inquisition was set up in the study to unmask the culprit. My father was the inquisitor. Had Gianchi done it? No, he replied, without hesitation. Had I done it? Well, if one was to be entirely truthful, the answer was complicated: I had been upstairs and had walked around Giampi's room, I said, and maybe, without realizing it, going by the table, had made the pen fall to the ground and break. This sounded then, as it sounds now, like a palpable lie. I should

181

have just said yes or no and left it at that. I was blamed, punished, and learned the crooked habit it has taken me a lifetime to break of not telling the truth to the extent that it would mislead or displease.

One August, we took a harrowing trip by car from Italy to Spain and I came down with the shivers. "*Your* sister is sick," one brother said to the other. We had taken to saying *your* father, *your* mother, *your* aunt, disowning relatives onto each other. Did we, already then, unaccustomed as we were to such proximity with our parents, find "the family," parents in the front, children in the back, oppressive? Driving up the mountains, the car stopped for lack of water in the radiator. We had each been given a leather water pouch with a toreador curtsying to a bull painted on it, and saved the day by offering up our water. Our behavior on the trip was being assessed by our father in points. I got a bicycle for my good points. Still, by the time we arrived in Palafrugell, I was sick. We checked into the hotel and I was put to bed, writhing with fever but pretending not to need a doctor. A doctor was summoned. In a fit of inspiration, I locked the door to my room from the inside and threw the key out the window. This delayed the torture, but in the end the aggravated, perspiring Spaniard was ushered to my bedside. He dug deep into a pocket and retrieved a used and crumpled handkerchief. He pulled up my nightshirt, flattened the handkerchief out on my chest, then laid his ear on it. It did not improve my opinion of doctors, or my flu.

Once a month, we drove to Switzerland to buy chocolate and cigarettes. On these occasions, I wore a blue dress with white Scotch terriers printed on it. A few years later, the special dress was a green and blue tartan check. My hair was cut short, "more practical," my mother said, neglecting to think of the impracticality, for one a decade old, of feeling like a thumb, naked, tufted, thrust in the face of the universe.

VI

There was a constant stream of architects at our house in Tokyo. Ettore Sottsass—I took a picture of him hugging one lustrous black shoe on his foot—and his wife Nanda Pivano, who had translated Masters' *Spoon River Anthology* and championed the Beat poets in Italy. I stared at her short blond hair, her pearl-lacquered short nails, pop-colored, op-patterned clothes. She sent me two pairs of patent leather shoes, one shocking pink, the other orange. I kept them in their box for a time, and took them out occasionally to sniff their smell of varnish and leather, and admire their impracticality. Years later when I was in boarding school in Florence, she sent me *The Tibetan Book of the Dead* and I made everyone laugh at the bit where one has to shout very loud into the dead man's ear. It was one of the books Nanda and I considered translating together. The other was an American dictionary of slang. But I only got around to two articles, one by Jerry Rubin, the other by Eldridge Cleaver, for *Pianeta Fresco,* the magazine that Ettore and Nanda were publishing together—a psychedelic pink and green flowery object you had to turn in different directions from page to page to read, and in which Ettore described for instance Nanda putting pistachio ice cream in the refrigerator instead of the freezer and the green cream dribbling down over the butter, the eggs, and the salad. They were proud of their undomesticity and it was what drew me to them. Every night, they ate at the Continental Hotel across from their apartment on the Via Manzoni in Milan, then they went to the movies. Every night. When I came up to visit them from boarding school, Nanda shouted to Ettore in the next room, "Did you see how pretty she's become?" Ettore drawled back, "I'll be right in there to make love to her." Nanda would lean forward conspiratorially, across the long wooden tray containing pebble-like candy divided into the colors of the rainbow, her face pink and blue from Ettore's fluorescent pink and blue phallic lamp nearby: "You are using the pill, I hope?" she'd say. I nodded yes, easier than explaining I wasn't even using sex.

Gio Ponti came to Japan and we met him at Frank Lloyd Wright's Imperial Hotel, many years before it was demolished. He put a single wobbly pearl like an uncertain drop of water into my palm and told stories of his wife: how she had filled a suitcase with potatoes from Venezuela and back in Milan had sent little parcels of them to her best friends with a note: "These are potatoes from Venezuela." When he met her, the first time, she cornered him, walking forward as he walked backwards, till his shoulders touched the wall, then she proffered her red lips and said, "Kiss me." Their daughter Lisa, on her first trip to Japan, was a widow who had two sons, ran her father's magazine *Domus,* and wore her hair up in a bun. She had a white beauty case—a hard pristine box with a single steel handle—called "zero." She was scared to sleep alone in the hotel so she came to stay with us and my father showed her a celadon cup with a curved bottom that could only be made to lie sideways on a shelf. He said, "You have to hold it," and placed it in her cupped hands. Magically, the hands separated, the cup dropped to the floor and shattered. For years after that episode, every time we visited her in Milan, Lisa would choose a Venini vase, thin as a membrane, a Tapio Wirkkala glass with an imprisoned bubble at the bottom of it, and give it to us, pleading, "Please break it, *please*."

On one of my visits, she had cut her hair very short and there was an artist in her kitchen who looked out the window and said in a lugubrious voice, "*Tedious* day," pausing between the words. Lisa sold a one-armed armchair by Mollino, who made chair seats in the shape of buttocks proffered for one to sit on, to a friend in New York and when she sent it, she wrapped a panettone with it because it was Christmas. The shipment arrived a month later, and the armchair had to be fumigated to remove the stench of decomposition.

The Japanese architect Kenzo Tange wore a little black bow tie and round-rimmed glasses like Le Corbusier and we went to visit the steel-winged cathedral he had just built. But architecture and design hadn't come into the house yet. What we had in Tokyo were remnants of Egypt—demure copies of demure periods of furniture: armchairs with curled wooden arms like fat little dancers poised for a pirouette, and round footstools embroidered in petit point. It was in Strada that weirdness and synthesis crept into the utilitarian, put there by my uncle Piero mostly, and received with enthusiasm by all: beanbags, rubber rocks one could sit on, plastic tubes with lights in them, leather armchairs in the shape of an open boxing glove, cubes. We learned to slump into, perch on, pat the new objects. Sometimes, carried away by his enthusiasm for the novel, my father went too far: he brought home eight ceramic stools in bright blue, red, and white, called "Chairs not to be sat on" because they had spikes, and holes, and ridges that made it torture to sit on them, though one always tried when there was nothing else.

186

They were scattered in the garden of la Casa Nova under bushes and my mother prayed they would be hit by lightning; one was, eventually, but was quickly glued back together by a zealous gardener.

In New York, we lived on Park Avenue, "that horrible street," my mother called it, and thought the building so stuffy she was not altogether displeased when it was discovered that the Italian cook from the Republic of San Martino had been dumping leftover spaghetti out the kitchen window.

Piero outdid himself there—Hulot would have approved. The living room, long as a bowling alley, was a soothing beige desert of dunes made of carpeted platforms and built-in couches, with a spiky palm to punctuate the mirage. There, I received my first job offer—to translate some texts of which I remember not a word, because I understood not a word, by Umberto Eco and Jean Baudrillard in semiotic times, for the Museum of Modern Art. The offerer, an Argentinian architect, said, to twist my arm, "I used to be involved in methodology, but not anymore: now I'm involved in meta-methodology." Flattered that he thought I understood, I accepted.

I went to work on a red "Valentine" typewriter designed by Sottsass, and as I was working one morning, another architect, Richard Meier, appeared, with his English friend Julia Bloomfield. When my parents left America, I went to live with them for a time and after overcoming the embarrassment of discussing what to do about my dirty laundry, and a few days later, that of having clogged a toilet in an apartment so white, I settled into developing pictures in the closet of my room, and in my spare time, watching a procession of architects sit in black leather Le Corbusier armchairs, eating at a white table painted with sixteen layers of lacquer, beneath a green and pink painting by Stella, a chicken whose skin Julia had cut, stuffed, and sewed back together with needle and thread. She has since lost both the recipe and the memory of that chicken.

When I left that last adolescent perch of received luxury, I learned about the architecture of the hovel at prices I could afford and diligently worked my way back up to those that I couldn't, obeying genetic impulse, I like to think.

If much of my life is spent worrying about paying the rent, it is because I live in an apartment that costs a small fortune every month, and I live in it because it has two large rooms with light and a terrace in a five-storey building. Twice in my life I lived in small places, one that cost very little, the other free: the first in Milan, a furnished flat, the second, a friend's guest room in Manhattan. I was very happy not "owning" anything and not having to identify with the place I lived in.

But my family, Alexandrians all of them, remonstrated both times: how could I live like that, didn't I want my own place, my own furniture? I was in a friend's guest room the color of a field mouse: stacks of paper on the floor—I was publishing a literary magazine—and a two-seat foam-rubber couch covered in grey corduroy that turned into an embracing bed, which in turn ate up a third of the room. I spoke on the phone sitting on the floor and leaning against the couch. I had light, a little table, a big noisy typewriter, a couple of bookshelves, a window from which I saw a row of brownstones across the street and a tree. All I had to pay was the telephone bill.

"You can't live like that."

But I did and liked it, and sometimes I miss it, miss the closest I ever came to not living alone after leaving home.

188

It made me anxious to look at apartments. Perhaps I sensed that my happy days free of financial responsibility were once again over. I was conscious of a certain resistance even when I saw the very apartment in which I have lived for a decade. In it, I have undergone a university of life. An Alexandrian will tell you it's a pied-à-terre. Having spent a number of years being ashamed of what I was paying for it, I now find it sufficient to make the payment in the first week of every month.

Bernard de Zogheb lives in a four-room apartment on the rue Djabarti in the *quartier grec* of Alexandria, with a terrace that made me think of Rome, I suppose because of the faded sienna wall on one side, and the view over a residential section of the city framed by a series of arches De Chirico might have drawn. His rent is one-tenth of mine. In New York a place like his might cost twice what I am paying for mine.

We both grew up in large houses. His has been converted into apartments. My family's is in ruins, at least half of it, and where the garden once was three apartment buildings and a mosque have been built. I calculated that about five hundred people live, and many more worship, where a dozen people, my family and their servants, once lived. It seems providential: I am glad I didn't inherit it; I could not have borne to sell it and I certainly would not have had the money to maintain it. The population of Alexandria is now five million. When I was a child it was barely a million.

With Bernard I went to see what used to be Cavafy's apartment on the rue de Lipsius, now a museum dedicated to him, with surprising new furniture he would never have chosen—a large brass bed with a green-and-crimson silk bedspread, ornately inlaid Egyptian chairs—his own furniture having been given, when he died, to a friend living in Athens. The walls are hung with black and white pictures of how the apartment actually was—a narrow bed, a white cotton bedspread, an old tired chair, books—that contradict one's every step into this "how it was." The Greek Consulate must have wanted to "improve" on the furniture since there was an opportunity of doing so, thinking perhaps to better justify the price of admission, or to show the poet off in a better light. There is no separation between what was supposed to be his house and the displays, between the man's life and the document of it, and there are no captions to indicate which is which. There are two bathrooms: one with a loo, one with a sink. They are very plain but too new to have been Cavafy's; but before realizing that, one has opened the door and wondered, "Is this where . . . ?"

Still, the place is the same place, with the same air coming through the window, the same inclination of light at the same hours, the same appearance of the seasons on his windowsill, the same traffic noises, somewhat intensified, the very same Greek Orthodox church, though the brothel and hospital—everything he said he needed to live on this very street—are now gone. The guard took the opportunity of our visit to ask if he could go and buy the newspaper. We agreed, but Bernard was shocked, thinking that there would be little left of the original manuscripts if visitors were allowed to remain alone with them.

I walked around as though I were going to rent the place, as though I were living in it already: six large rooms, high ceilings, a view of the street and trees, no tall buildings, light from every window. All I could think was, for this he probably paid twenty Egyptian pounds or less a month, about seven dollars. It was not considered grand by any means, neither the size of it nor the area it is in. Just acceptable. I don't know of many apartments as beautiful as that in New York, really.

I worry that there is never quite enough money, though somehow there is always just enough. I run up a steady trickle of debt with my credit card. I paid it off two years ago and vowed never to use it again, but little by little, the debt has reformed, or rather, I have caused it to. The bank wrote me a letter, recently, congratulating me on how well I was "managing" my account. In fact, they are pleased at how well I am mismanaging it.

For each person God devises an economy that will best oppress them, in the range from too little to too much, from nothing to everything. Very little and just enough are appealing prospects. To write this book I was given an advance that amounts to what I earn for a few articles. Writing is writing. I don't save the good head for the book and give the bad one over to articles. I start from the same confusion and wait for it to clear up, in both cases. The relationship between finishing and money is closer with the articles, but money is essential to the book: not the amount, but the fact *that one is paid to write*—a comfort through barren hours. One is assured of three readers at least, including oneself, and that is all the assurance one needs to begin. Continuing is another matter, no longer anyone's business but one's own, or rather the book's.

The shops would close if they had to rely on the likes of me, though grocery stores would survive. The Alexandrian in me who will give up every luxury for the luxury of space and light in the only, though derelict, cosmopolitan city in the world also makes me like people to come and eat at my house often, though the quality of the spirits has fluctuated over the years.

Like my grandmother Berthe, who gathered all the Alexandrian strays on Sunday for lunch, I have people for lunch on Sundays—did so even before I knew she had done so. My other grandmother, Rebecca, the one from Izmir, when she was still living in Rhodes had a minimum of a dozen people at her table at every meal.

Pierre the priest made a list of all the houses where he could go and stay if he felt too old to live by himself. He worked out that he would stay about a month in each, and with twelve alternating hosts he would never have to stay with anyone more than once a year. If I wanted to visit all the family houses, I could do so, probably for years without even running into any of the owners. For they have built, bought, and refurbished places by seas, by lakes, and lagoons, in cities, forests, and open countryside, as though to guarantee their own permanence. Those houses are heated, staffed, maintained. The beds are made, there are clean towels in the bathroom, enough in the refrigerator to have breakfast on.

The guest room at Piero and Beppe's house in Milan: on the walls, a fabric printed with pomegranates, demurely closed, then erupting obscenely into red flowers the size of cabbages. Watercolors of Lake Como, one with a pensive young man gazing at the lake; nymphs dancing naked; a lady strutting in her 1800s finery, a dwarf in turban picking up the train of her gown, a monkey in pleated collar holding up a mirror from which she coquettishly appears to be averting her gaze, as though daring the reflection to come to her; a crayon drawing of a setter; a pen sketch of an Egyptian temple; a Moor in a yellow turban; a bearded Ottoman soldier in a red fez. On the side table, a sloped writing desk on which to write two words on a business card, bearing three bill clasps in the shape of hands; three bronze dachshunds on a marble lampstand, the blown iridescent glass lampshade modeled on an overturned buttercup. Above the twin beds a long-haired maiden casting saucer eyes up to heaven, and above the oval frame an olive branch, replaced every Easter.

On Beppe's pea-green corduroy armchair, a green velvet cushion with the embroidered words, "It's so expensive to be rich." Below, the sounds of the two wire-haired dachshunds, Ambra and Agata, and of Dolly, the ruling housekeeper from the Philippines no one dares to cross: on the frailest frame, lashless black almond eyes in a pretty face. A Moroccan manservant in livery—her slave and victim—cleans, dusts what appears to be spotless. They are preparing dinner for thirty. Who are these thirty people, I inquire of Beppe, and he replies, "All your relatives . . . ," but he thinks it over, then adds, "My nephew is coming with his wife."

I always found Piero's house more welcoming than any I knew, Beppe more soothing than any mother, more playful than any friend. Piero was the first in the family to eye me with interest, to unabashedly appreciate me. Escape, while I was at Poggio Imperiale, meant boarding a fast train to Milan and going to stay with him. I usually left with a group of comrades. We boarded the train looking like gaunt novices in our uniforms, and emerged from the lavatory in false eyelashes, miniskirts, zippered blousons.

In Milan, silver boxes were filled with Benson & Hedges and Kent cigarettes I could smoke to my heart's content. In the daytime, when they went to work—Piero at eight, Beppe later after an elaborate ritual of face creams, bath, shaving, choosing suit, tie, shirt—I was free to roam around the mirrored biscuit-colored penthouse with a terrace all around it, make phone calls, take showers, smoke and smoke, get dressed for dinner.

Piero and Beppe, who were known as *il* (meaning "the") in Milan, Piero being the little *i* and Beppe the tall *l,* never had any plan they demanded I adhere to, unlike school, unlike my parents. They just asked whether I wanted to have dinner with them, and it was understood that I could do as I pleased. If we had lunch at home, we sat at individual folding tables, and Wally, their housekeeper at the time, had such a hallowed regard for my uncle's time that she tied three or four cherries together invisibly with black string so that he would not have to waste time picking them up one at a time. He never even noticed, and had he done so would have disapproved.

Ever since I can remember, I was attracted to the polite lawlessness that Piero and Beppe practiced. Unlike families, they had no routines. They invented a living for themselves: Beppe represented fashion companies of various sorts, Piero designed houses, boats, castles, mostly for wealthy people, usually dealing with the women. He fell under their spell and for a time inhabited their life, discovered their innermost propensities.

Invariably, he made them out to be lapidary. He was entertained by them, as though they were prodigies. He distilled them for me. One client punctuated every expression of disapproval saying, "Ridiculous and pretentious!" It was so satisfying we took to saying it at the least provocation. Another told of having gone into an elegant shop on Via della Spiga in Milan and of having been ignored by the saleslady; she kept repeating dumbfounded, "And I *had* my Vuitton bag!" That, too, became our saying for incomprehensible situations. A dapper lady journalist Piero and Beppe took everywhere with them—to Varese, to Monte Marcello, to Venice—once remarked after a boat ride along the Ligurian coast that had lasted the whole day, "Too much sun!" It became proverbial to describe anyone or anything excessive. It had to be said in a squeak. A lady from Torino, always sheathed in beige étamines and cashmeres, was baptized "the dearly departed," as were all the bland people we encountered from then on.

It was in the seventies that Piero and Beppe bought an oil mill in the little town of Monte Marcello, on whose narrow cobbled streets cars were not allowed. It was once a fishermen's village—now mostly populated by women and old people—and its houses were painted all shades of pastel—light yellows, pinks, russets, with green wooden shutters. They were built on a concentric pattern with a tower outside the walled perimeters of the town. Piero and Beppe's house looked like a pink sliver on three floors from the outside, but once inside there was a very long living room with a curving white wall to one side, a black couch snaking along the full astonishing length of it made of covered foam rubber, cut to resemble a curvy coast; a slate table, Japanese inkwells for ashtrays, white tiles on the floor, a zebra skin. In those days, Piero and Beppe wore a great deal of white and black, with an occasional red belt or red espadrilles.

Black and white were the three guest rooms, too, except for the one with double-decker beds off the kitchen that was apple green. I slept there many times and loved the scent of lavender in my nostrils in the morning that wafted in from the terrace. The room with a double bed and zebra-print bedspread facing the little garden was given to the guest, or guests, of honor—to the "couple" in residence.

One couple, who had long awaited their tryst found passion thwarted when the man caught his penis in the zipper of his trousers. Further humiliation awaited him at the hands of a hospital orderly who would not dignify the injury with anything more than a band-aid. Another pair, who addressed each other invariably as "My treasure" no matter what the tone of the preceding sentence, had bloody fights that resounded all over the town's stone congregation. One day, the woman yelled at the man, "Fuck you, my treasure!" and that too we enthusiastically appropriated for our lexicon.

Speculation on the sexual affairs of others was one of the pastimes of Monte Marcello. As for the hosts, they had a harbor of transient ships nearby. La Spezia was also the place where Beppe went for certain delicacies such as the *torta pasqualina,* a tart made of spinach, ricotta cheese, and hardboiled eggs in a pastry. In the summer throngs of people came to dinner, sometimes thirty or forty of them. It meant Beppe had to spend the day shopping and preparing. Any crisis on which Beppe consulted Piero would be shelved by Piero's saying, "Do as you please." With this motto, he guarded his peace.

An old russet-haired yellow-eyed woman called Brillantina, our neighbor in between her spells at the lunatic asylum, liked to harangue Beppe whose pink terrace overlooking the top of the bell tower bordered hers. He emerged one morning from his bedroom and saw her squatting over a bucket. She yelled belligerently, "I'll do it, I'll do it, then I'll throw it in your face!" Even one less finicky than Beppe would have retreated. We were convinced that she did this to attract his attention.

With the priest, Brillantina had a more complicated liaison.

She despised him on principle for being a priest, and hated that his little piece of land should be right under her nose, across the narrow road. He had a little orchard there which he visited at dusk. It was on one of these occasions that she began to throw ripe figs at him from the branches of the tree that reached her perch. But soon this retribution no longer sufficed and she sought to put her rage into words. Being illiterate she could not write to him herself. In town, there was a writer from Milan, a novelist, who regularly rented a flat. Brillantina turned up at his doorstep but he was dismayed to discover that she didn't want him to word the missive, only to pen it at her dictation.

The other éminence grise of the town was an eccentric Irishwoman who had married an Italian diplomat. She had a talent for manipulating the town's politics away from the defacements of "modernization." She made sure the right lampposts were put up, that no ugly buildings were built. For years after her husband's death, she had continued to inhabit the tower, but as her finances dwindled she sold it, and after various transitions ended up in a tiny stone house in the middle of a field whose stony earth she soon coaxed into harboring rose bushes. She had a sister who came to visit on occasion and had only two loves—Haile Selassie of whom she said that he spent his nights circling the heavens in a plane for fear of being assassinated, and Addis Ababa—and when it was damp at night and we strayed out into the garden at the tower, she would say, "It's all very well for you young people who don't suffer from hemorrhoids to sit in the damp." In describing a daughter-in-law, one sister attempted diplomacy while the other suddenly blurted, "Let's face it, she's a real *cook*." Anyone we didn't like became a *real cook*.

The real cook at Piero and Beppe's was a villager in her eighties, once the town beauty. Maria had snowy hair, a long tanned face and turquoise eyes, and her dream was to build herself a brand-new house outside the village and abandon her old pink one just past the arch through which one entered the town. She looked astonished morning till night, and she may well have been—until a few years before she had never left Monte Marcello, nor talked to anyone she hadn't known since her birth or theirs. Almost certainly, she had never heard the word "diet," with which every dinner conversation, as we sat on tall Chinese chairs surrounded by walls hung with blue and white Portuguese tiles, was filled.

We swung violently from feast to famine. One way or the other, food, or the lack of it, was never far from anyone's thoughts. An enormous dinner would be countered, on the following day at lunchtime, by a hard-boiled egg and a tomato. This austere picnic was packed into a hamper and taken aboard a roomy wooden boat, inexplicably named *Topsy* by its previous owner; it had been built in Naples and its prow had been transformed by my uncle into a communal bed consisting of white vinyl cushions covered with large brown towels that were replaced every day.

In those days in Italy tanning was a mania men and women alike subjected themselves to rigorously—the women topless and the men in little cotton slips with a clasp on the side that when unclasped permitted the sun to visit even that last oasis. Anastasia, a guest who was considered part of the so-called family, was recognized by all as the specialist of suntans: she went around pointing out to people the areas they had over-looked. "Turn over on your stomach," she would order, "you are white as a worm on your back." She herself, who had a lean boyish figure, could lie in the most ingenious positions to achieve an integral tan; her specialty was the sideways position for which she would lie on one hip, both shoulders on the ground, arms stretched back so the armpits could get brown, and the legs bent so the sun would hit the inner thigh of one leg and the outer thigh of the other, which after fifteen minutes precisely she would reverse.

She was horrified at the one-piece bathing suit I wore on my first visit and soon squeezed me into a pink and white cotton polka-dot string bikini she had bought in Portofino. I was forbidden to wear the top. Coming from a strict boarding school where I had worn a scratchy grey wool skirt and pullover and a starched pleated white collar, I felt like a tied-up roast in a butcher's display case, but soon became accustomed to it. After interminable exposures in the sun, we would take long showers, then spend an hour at least putting on cream.

Anastasia's sexual exploits were the subject of her own conversation primarily. She loved sex, changed lovers as often as a tempting one appeared on the horizon, remained friends with all of them. Once my brother slipped on a nail on the deck of *Topsy* and made a gash in the sole of his foot. It was bandaged and he had to keep his foot propped up on a table. When it came time for us to go out to dinner, Anastasia offered to keep him company. In the course of the night, we were told over breakfast by Anastasia herself, there had been a thunderstorm and this had brought her solicitously to the patient's bedside. "*Badajdoomfete!*" my uncle yelled triumphantly—it was the onomatopoeic word he had invented to describe the sound of two bodies colliding. It was understood with Anastasia that nothing binding was intended.

When Piero and Beppe sold the house in Monte Marcello,

199

they scoured the exotic world every summer for a house they could rent that would send their senses reeling: a red wooden villa on the Bosporus, a castle in Sicily, a modernist mirage in the south of Portugal. They took with them their diets, linens, languors and a little court of noblewomen and musicians, crime writers and creatures of fashion—their family in the line of beauty.

Piero had me invited to my first ball, at the Villa d'Este, and arranged for me to buy a dress from his friend, the designer Ken Scott, who was then very popular in Milan for his flower prints. The dress was a long silk jersey shift of pink and mauve hydrangeas so large that one flower covered my entire chest; the openings for the neck and arms were embroidered with cascades of colored glass beads. The dress very much resembled Ken Scott's terrace of pink and red zinnias, which I would some ten years later overlook from a little apartment I rented— part of a house that belonged to him and where one night I heard him yell for my benefit, "Get out, leave this horrible town, or you'll get stuck like me!"

The dress did not suit me and I remember well the nothing that happened to me at Villa d' Este that night. But still, I had been taken into the world and at least formed an idea of it.

Something made Piero adopt me and I him. I could not know then that I was attracted to Piero's independence, infatuated with his sibylline ways, his finding the amusing thing to do without appearing to do anything out of the ordinary. There were times one knew to tiptoe around him—during his afternoon naps for instance.

He was, and is, punctiliously groomed: a tanned dome, hair

cropped to a millimeter before the curl can develop, a checked shirt, a suit made by the tailor Caraceni (it is Beppe who sees to it that their wardrobes are replenished, that the cut is updated and the tailor instructed), the colored cord holding up reading glasses, shining almond-shaped black eyes casting about mischievously, tricorn lips drawn up at the corners.

Piero opened for me the doors of many houses, my favorite ones being his. They never contained the dusty relics, messy bathrooms, oppressive dining rooms of family life. He refurbished them as though lining a coat. He and Beppe loved to displace furniture from one house to another. At one time, they had a little apartment up a terrifying staircase on Piazza del Parlamento in Rome. In it was a painted screen depicting a view of the city, with little windows along the façades of buildings that were lit from behind. That screen is now in their house in Milan. We called this game of speculating on what to sell, what to buy and what to move from one place to another "monopoly." Piero and Beppe always made enough to live well and one felt that more was gaily frittered away than was accumulated.

All this I unconsciously admired—the self-determination, the turning of life into anecdote, and anecdote into language, so that an expression we used at any time among ourselves, once remembered, could recall precisely the atmosphere of all that had surrounded it.

Clothes and my aunt Mariuccia. I remember her thin legs in veiled white stockings, the first time I saw her, the fine blue leather shoes with a rectangular point, already then the bangs, straight hair to just below the jaw—the feminist helmet: severe and stylish. It was in the sixties, in our little town called, disobligingly, Buguggiate. The ionized air from the lake nearby, if it made my grandmother jittery, left Mariuccia calm, in command of her faculties, and of her relatives-to-be: us. She was my uncle Aldo's new and accomplished wife and she had her own business, called Krizia, after a dialogue by Plato on the vanity of women; she had been a teacher, born in the Gallic hilltop town of Bergamo. She was the first woman in Italy to have a line of ready-to-wear, and she had begun in 1954.

Around the time I started to take an interest in clothes, she began to take an interest in those I wore. She would finger a collar, a sleeve. "What is this?" she would ask sternly. "Biba," or, "Portobello Road," I replied defiantly, pleased she had noticed. It was important not to appear to like her designs too much, or it would become a family dictate to wear them. I know now that she inspects every single thing she sees, scavenging for a bone of an idea she might use in her next collection—for men, children, beds, bathrooms, the women with and in them.

I wore her clothes but not always in the way she had intended them. The first was a trapeze-shaped cardigan in shiny silver-grey silk knit, with a wide ribbed border, narrow sleeves, flared at the cuffs, so delicate a bitten nail could pull a thread. There was a time, lasting several years, when she made long and narrow printed scarves to be wound once around the neck, then left to hang like a priest's stole, a tape measure, or the cords of a stethoscope. I had one of green and red rhomboids on a parchment-colored background. I wore it over a long sweater with wooden buttons, in a wavy weave like knitted hay and grass with thistles caught in it, and a greenish flannel skirt to the ankles; it earned me the nickname "The Big Droop," from a friend who shared my office at the Museum of Modern Art, overlooking Picasso's goat.

I went to meet a man who had written a book titled *Venice, Frail Barrier,* and I, too, was a frail barrier as far as he was concerned. It took many hours to dress for the occasion. Finally, in a series of gossamer layers, I was a fragment from a skating rink, skated on, white and flurried at the edges, in palest water-blue wool pants and flapping jacket, crêpe shirt printed with fluttering wings. I lay on a couch covered in striped Moroccan rugs, fell asleep; a black-and-white picture was taken and titled "Reefer Madness." Fashion can be that, I suppose: a period piece made of nothings added together—smoke, sofa, the moment, a length of wool, one of silk, a shade of blue. When I returned to Italy, I received a little note from my uncle saying that since I was now living in Milan, there was not much point in my wearing their clothes any more. Implying that my life had lost whatever visibility it had once had.

Some time later, I went to work for another designer. The Japanese year. The Amish. The Harem. Etamine, nubuk, twill. I learned words. Used them in his favor. Learned that clothes must fit a man, and a woman must fit the clothes. I heard him say of models, "She has a neck like a giraffe . . . the face of a monkey . . . the hips of an elephant." Discrimination against the shape of a body or that of an animal. By the time I left, I had exhausted the very idea of glamour.

Mariuccia chose blue-green for every piece of paper at her club in the Caribbean to match the color of the sea. It is a reserve described by one man as a place where you pay "*not* to have television, *not* to hear children, *not* to get the newspapers." The only town on the island, called Codrington, is not close enough to walk to, and has fifteen hundred inhabitants, of which only a dozen are visible. There is one grocery store and several bars.

At a thousand dollars a night, the little house on the beach comes with the sensation that one will not have it for long. (Truman comes in to check the refrigerator on the veranda—he is a nurse administering objects of desire.) As Mariuccia herself said, "It's a thousand dollars a night, then everything you touch is seventy dollars." She herself is shocked by the prices.

A bungalow on a white sandy beach deserted by all except the certainty of luxury before and after submersions in cerulean waters, though the library is free. She never stops running about, running things; fusses about the number of towels, the cooking time of string beans, the crease in a tablecloth, the whiteness of uniforms. Aldo takes off in his golf cart and pretends to be on holiday an hour a day.

Lester Bird, prime minister of the Republic of Antigua, Redonda, and Barbuda, in a purple polo shirt, and his friend walk towards the main building, hand in hand. He played golf with Aldo this morning. Every night before going to sleep he practices his swing on the floor of the bedroom, and every morning when he wakes up.

Mariuccia, king of at least one part of the island, came into the water, long-limbed, pale-eyed, an imperious, feminine sword. A man indicted in the Italian Socialist party bribery scandal was coming to lunch, she announced. When she had met him in Milan, every time she had mentioned a hotel, clinic, restaurant, he had said in a low voice, "Mine." "Well, I told him, yours or not, the clinic stinks, *fa schifo,*" Mariuccia says she told him. "He said I would never make any money on my hotel in the Caribbean. But at least it's a beautiful thing."

The indicted man's wife, Lella, when they arrived, wore a gold man-sized Rolex watch, with little diamonds all around the face of it, and on her finger a gold-mounted diamond the size of a grape. Around her neck, a string of brightly colored geometric plastic shapes, such as children play with. "I have convinced Salvatore that everything must be done with love, whether it's cooking or running a three-thousand-bed hotel." She had small lively green eyes, a furrowed brow, hair streaked blond, as so many Italian women like to wear it. She was stocky and direct. "Salvatore is calm itself; imagine if you and I had gotten together," she said to Aldo, who was a little startled by the intimacy of this conjecture. "He always tells me to calm down."

"I travel so much," Salvatore said by way of an explanation. "Do you know what a good hotel manager should do?" he asked, eager to impart his knowledge. "He should sleep in a different room of the hotel every night to see if the shower is leaking, or the closet needs hangers. He shouldn't trust anyone to do their job."

Later he said, "I left Sicily because it was like a village, everyone discussing who had put a wall up where and whether he should be allowed to, and now Milan has become like that . . . I blame everything on the former mayor of Milan. I knew nothing directly of the case I was implicated in. That's why I appeared in court."

"I don't know whether that was the right thing to do," Lella chided.

They had grilled barracuda on flattened leaves of steamed spinach arranged in the shape of a flower, then milles feuilles, lemon cream pie, tarte tatin, espresso. The food was better here, they declared, than at the St. James Club in Antigua, though they liked the choice of "three waters there: a calm sea on one side, a wild sea on the other, the swimming pool."

Salvatore is a small man, bald, white hair at the temples, hazel eyes, and a full mouth. "It's all Negroes in the government here, right?"

"Yes," Aldo said, "it's a republic that has been under the same rule for ages."

VII

A friend said that my father lives in an artist's garret. My father says it is a sacrifice to live in such a small space and does not take kindly to my suggestion that "two hearts, one hut" is a formula for happiness. Did he give up the houses he built and the way in which he inhabited them because he no longer identified with that impersonation of himself? Did that performance, one he maintained for my mother, demand too much of him? Was she the stronger, the one for whom no one could ever be too strong, since she labeled herself weak? Perhaps he tried to give her back her parents' house in Alexandria all his life and she took it for granted. But then the universe we grew up in was one that she painted, and she has re-formed like a worm of which a segment had been severed.

When my parents' marriage stopped, as irrevocably as a performance stops, after the initial shock wore off, she said it was like taking off a pair of shoes that were too tight. Those shoes were a constant fear of his anger. For him, the new woman was like putting on a pair of slippers, for my mother is despotic in her implicit demand that others be brave at all times. Was it the habits of his marriage he escaped from—the rules he himself had set for himself, that he had religiously adhered to so as to please and not to displease my mother and his ideal of himself, the things he believed ought to be admired, when he was young? She, the witness, inured to his valor, taking it for granted, made it impossible for him to go back into the comfort of his own more human skin. So the sign of falling in love with his true self, after falling out of love with his ideal one, was to say one day, unexpectedly, "I hate classical music."

Adultery is the mostly invisible web on which our lives have been woven: my father's, mine, my mother's (without her consent), her own parents'. Adultery was the pastime in Alexandria and it would have been hard to determine, such is the nature of adultery, who, exactly, was being untrue to whom. Even a virtuous lady, pitied for having married an unattractive though wealthy man, conducted a twenty-year love affair with a Greek gentleman, right in Alexandria, under the very nose of her own righteousness and of a society that considered her above suspicion.

There was the surprise of hearing my mother denigrate my father, an example of justice and perfection she had upheld to us every day with her every gesture of devotion and unquestioning fidelity. Like one dusting a relic, or watering a plant, she was the curator of his superiority in the human race, and like any devoted servant, thought very little of the not-hims—the world being a radiant him with greyish slivers of not-hims: idiots, poor things, unlucky, misguided beings. She denigrated him for having left her for a younger woman, but in her heart of hearts, and out loud, forgave him, never even considered him guilty, since it was she, *that woman*, who had broken up their forty-five-year marriage. For if he were to blame, why had she dedicated her life to an impostor? That would make him a liar and her an idiot. It was a lesser evil, a smaller loss, to consider that he had been ensnared by the new woman's younger wiles. The fact is that Cristina was looking for a man to protect her and found one, in the bosom of the family. She chose well: my father is an honorable man. Having tipped the entire order of his existence, physiologically, geographically, and being pragmatic, moved by reason as he thinks himself to be, he will consolidate the tremors of instinct with ethical action so as to annul, little by little, any fragrance of lust or willfulness that may reach the nostrils of society, and his own much more critical ones.

I, the daughter, listening to my mother's confidences, was "the other woman" in my own life and so the villain of her piece, as well as her confidante. I had to see "the other woman's" point. Let's say I saw it very well and was moved to defend her, now and again. I said, there is no fault. I said, out of habit you thought you were happy. You were, in fact, occupied. Dear mother, you lived with one man for nearly half a century and that's more company and more of a marriage than most people have in several lifetimes; it lasted so long it had to degenerate into its opposite. Isn't that the nature of things? But there are no reasons, only chance.

A woman in Chianti said, "The heat, when there is no shade, robs you of all sentiment." A definition of marriage, perhaps, of my parents' marriage, certainly, before the breakup. My own "marriage" has been graced with a great deal of shade. If I have been with X for nine years, they were not like nine of the years my mother had with my father because, counting up the days and the hours, you wouldn't get more than three months if one excludes the time spent on the phone, a virtual being together, averaging six hours a week, which comes to about one day a month and so, twelve days a year multiplied by nine, equal in itself to three months. Total, between real and virtual hours: six months. But in these "years," we have been together in the time I have set aside for him and he has set aside for me. We have worked, eaten, slept, often, suspended as though in the same amniotic sac. He is a place I inhabit naturally like the air between my fingers.

A friend said of a writer, "His first book is brilliant, but now he is going to have to take on the subject of sex." I thought I might soon come under the same invisible guidelines of what does or doesn't constitute a writer's duties. The bed from which I write could tell what it has seen. I think myself lucky, and so, am. As to the detail, of what possible use can it be when being there is the only prerequisite of eros? A man I knew once said, "Eroticism is mute." I adopted it. If I let the pen run everywhere, in and out of me, from my memory to my eyes to my hands, from the senses of the past to those of the present, a sum of everything remembered till this moment when I say, "I remember," I must leave, for now, at least one patch of uncultivated ground on which to stand while I write—eros, the key to my coming not so much of age as of myself, a tremor that shakes hidden recesses open.

That I know who I am is clearly proved by the fact that I have no clear idea of what that is, other than the sensation within any given moment. The only course of blood I can honestly say I feel running through my veins is the desire to understand and to make a record of the journey. English does not forgive abstraction or the putting of dots on every ego *i*. I see as I write.

My parents broke up once when he was still in his teens because he felt they were too young to get married. It might have been his way of withdrawing while maintaining both his and her honor intact, without saying either that he did not love her or that he did not want to marry her. Perhaps he did not even know what he felt. But his sister Sarah stepped into the picture; my mother had confided in her: she was as unhappy as a nineteen-year-old can be when a love affair has ended. It is only twenty years after the danger is past that one begins to experience waves of gratitude for all those one did *not* marry. His father's eyes shone, someone said, because she was wealthy and higher up on the social ladder, as the Tilches had been with regard to the Pintos a few decades earlier, when my grandparents met. And so they were married, but were they in love, and does it matter, considering they were in something together for nearly half a century, and it isn't over, no matter who lives where? They had three children—that is all that history will record: genetic continuity, and so, memory.

Now my father wishes to apply "falling in love" as a cure to any ill. When did he become a romantic? To a friend suffering a depression, he said, "It is because you haven't met true love yet." Little does he care that the definition of love varies greatly and that in the case of this friend it consists, for instance, of a measure of sadism, a measure of masochism, and no love ever greater than that which he has for his mother who crushes the breath out of him and without whom he fears he will be destroyed as a writer and as a man. She is his "true love," if that can be measured at least by intensity, if in no other way. But my father still simplifies his perceptions to the point of interchangeability, so that he sees what he is undergoing now as

211

"true love," whereas it is his *me* expanding at last like a drop in an ocean. A friend, who has watched him extend protection to multitudes of "poor things" in the past, sees him now as openly espousing his ambitions and desires for the first time in his life. There is no blaming him.

To see my mother as ruler of the marriage, for a change. Did her strength torment him all his life? I remember him saying once that she never just put her arms around him and hugged him. I remember trying to pull her down to sit on my bed in Tokyo—I was perhaps twelve—she was confectioned in a black sleeveless Cardin dress with a white camellia in the fold of her décolleté, smelling of Madame Rochas, ready to go out with him for dinner, and she put her palms up in front of her chest to fend off my embrace so I wouldn't tousle her hair: short, high at the crown and sides, teased, combed and lacquered, with an invisible side part, one lock coaxed over one brow.

How does she view adversity? I think as a prerogative of the weak or as the result of bad luck. But the good is inseparable from the bad and all of it tourism for internal eyes.

In Milan, five days before my second trip to Egypt, Piero and Beppe's guests spoke of diets and they all appeared to be failures, as year after year I observed that not one of those diet talkers, who had always just tried a new diet, were about to begin one, knew someone who had, smoked to stay thin, was ever any thinner, though I am sure there was never a single day when they did not wake up with the thought of having to lose weight or of having gained it, usually both together, excluding the three days a year graced with the knowledge of a kilo lost.

Cairo. This room at the Atlas Hotel in Zamalek, with its white formica furnishings, only takes me back to the seventies instead of my childhood for which I have come in search. I am on the seventh floor. The city below, veiled in golden soot: a stadium, a mosque, a row of shuttered stores no one does business in. The dirt is exotic, dust from the desert. A plastic shield around the light switch by the door protects the wall from fingerprints.

I see two men crossing the street, their grey and beige galabiyas progressively darker towards the hem. The edges of the sidewalk are caked with old dust, a rubbish bin is surrounded by what didn't make it into it. Sunny day, yellow sky, I can taste the car exhaust fumes and the fumes from cement factories by the Pyramids.

The solace of a Chopin nocturne heard in this room, and on a scratchy radio at the store where I bought film.

How can I find any place exotic when I am surrounded by my own place, the body, wherever I go? I wake up, see I need to cut my toenails; what could be more familiar than my own feet, my hands, the body I bathe every day, my face. I live in this organism, the country I come with. In it I am at home and the foreign is not foreign, though sometimes, as in times of illness, my body feels as though nothing could be more alien.

The story ends and begins again with a glass of water after a night of thirst and physical pain that obscured mental anguish, any sentimentality regarding the loss of a child—expulsion of the animal-child. Do they ever not look mongoloid? Could you ever mistake one for an ordinary child? I wondered, when I considered keeping it. He never leaves you until he dies, until you die or unless you kill him, "for his own good": they have weak hearts, only grow to be about thirty years old, sickly. N. had two, she thought of no one else. Why should anyone mind?

I saw him on the screen of a sonogram: he had two legs, two feet, two arms, a torso, a chest, a head, ears even, and orbs where his eyes lived before they died. He moved about like an unsuspecting tadpole as they measured the length of his spine, from the base of the skull to the coccyx, from the top of the head to the tips of the toes, from the shoulder to the wrist. He opened his mouth and inhaled amniotic fluid; he waved his hands in semicircles, like a swimmer staying afloat. If he was a freak, he was a freak locked in the body of an ordinary human being. He looked as he should, moved as he should, at the age of four months before birth.

Others don't want you to dedicate yourself to a mongoloid. Isn't it a fascist ideal to only dedicate yourself to something of a superior, or at least standard, nature? I toyed with the idea of keeping this child to contradict that, partly, and because I had not dedicated myself to myself yet. But I still lacked the courage to leave once and for all the standard life, itself a monstrosity—the very one I now feel I must guard against. It blinded me for at least twenty years of my adult existence and I am not saying it doesn't do so now, here and there, in delicate ways at moments when I still feel it is a strange woman who doesn't have a child, and at moments—few, out of all the ones in a day—that it is unnatural to be so by oneself, day after day: usually on Sundays, on waking. Yet my dislike for Sundays began when as a child there was no getting away from one or another member of the family. Still, the doubt persists, like a tourist uninterested in the site: what would it have been like with someone I had chosen? Or had had assigned to me. I had not chosen this creature in the form it—he—took. Should I have kept him? How different am I from neo-Nazis beating up deaf children in their desire to eliminate deformity? I suppose different in that I did not want the creature to experience discrimination, my own, first and foremost.

The kindly "genetic advisers" in hospitals would like every parent to have a "perfect child," and would, having sighted an abnormality, advise them to "terminate the pregnancy," a euphemism for "killing" the abnormal fetus. I'm all for abortion when a mother, a father, feel they cannot have a child, but because the child is imperfect? It is discrimination—elegant, accepted, widespread, middlebrow.

It was a Tuesday morning. I got up and for once did not manage to put the right foot on the ground before the left, as the Chinese believe one should. I was packing to go to Greece with X. I thought I would telephone the hospital for the result of the test I had been subjected to two weeks earlier—an injection at the top of my growing belly to withdraw two phials of amniotic fluid: "You will feel a little prick, now," the Swedish doctor had said just before he had inserted the needle. That was the second test I had had, in the deluded hope that the first might be wrong. Of course I wanted a miracle and received one. If anyone had told me that it is when you lose *the thought* dearest to you that you feel for the first time awake, I would have wanted to keep that possibility away, I would have considered having been told a curse, would have wished I had never heard.

A standard mother wants a standard child. The mirror in

which I saw myself reflected was broken the instant I knew I had conceived a mongoloid: if I didn't want a flawed, retarded reflection of myself, why should I want any reflection at all? To think of having a child is to consider the expansion of one's empire, in the idiot sense of a "grip" on the world. To be told that the empire is about to contract (though in the eyes of the world only) is to enter the inner chamber—one door leads to a room, which leads to a room, which leads to a room, and the outside becomes clearer without effort as the lens is adjusted from within. When the diagnosis was confirmed the decision, though predictable, was not yet made. When made, in the light of my fear, the child had to be aborted.

One doctor, in a low-ceilinged white office lined with black and white pictures of himself as a younger, jovial man in a white mask pulling viscid babies from between feet in stirrups, described the "procedure": it takes fourteen to sixteen hours; you are given a pill to start contractions; after about an hour the dose is repeated, and the medication makes you nauseous; if the contractions become unbearable you get a very mild pain-killer—you don't want the contractions to stop, though—then another dose; and so on until, in alternate contractions and retchings, you rupture the amniotic sac; now you are ready to give birth to the baby, who has by now been asphyxiated by the frequency of the contractions; he will be born dead, you are assured, and will be taken away in a basin.

It was a white kidney-shaped enamel basin and the nurse took it away, covering it with a folded disposable blue plastic mattress shield, just as the priest at Mass covers the chalice, as though some alchemy were to take place for which secrecy and an absence of light were required. I had checked into the hos-pital at midday. By two I was in labor. By ten I would have given anything to have it stop, to leave my body at war with itself. Even a chip of ice melted in the mouth brought on violent convulsions. I pushed a wave out, it receded, I pushed again . . . at the thirteenth hour, the waters broke—a sense of relief. More contractions produced the rubbery little being, *my boy*, an embryo in the fifth month—he slipped out, incongruously willing, easily, as though he'd waited for the opportunity. I felt well in every cell of my body as though every brooding particle of bile had been lifted away, like evaporated dew. I felt nothing. There was a white polystyrene cup by the bed and a mustard yellow pitcher of iced water. I filled the glass, drank the water, felt the clean chill of it in my mouth and in my throat, then sleep coming over me like a black velvet cloak pulled down over the universe.

To think one belongs in a family is the first obstacle to stripping one's identity to the core that sways by itself whichever way it pleases.

I returned to Alexandria and to the cemetery, with Madame Cristina's helper, Tasula, who buys the Elite's daily provisions at the market. We went to cemetery number three at Chatby, and did the prerequisite hopping about from tomb to tomb, in search of my grandparents'. But Tasula, at least, had some idea of where they were, having brought flowers there on behalf of Madame Cristina—an extraordinarily touching gesture, made, as it was, knowing that it would in all likelihood remain unacknowledged.

I was taking a photograph of a stray dog stretched comfortably on a tombstone, above his head a row of colorful clothes hung out to dry. When I turned around, I noticed at my heels the name "Rebecca Alhadeff." To her right, partly obscured by a patina of dust and rain, "Isaac Alhadeff." A tree had originally been planted on the side of the graves. It had grown so much that its roots had pulled up the low railing around the two graves.

The young keeper, son of the man in charge, summarily cleared the graves of some of the weeds, overturned a bucket of water over one slab, then the other, rubbed off some of the dirt, then gracefully deposited two ot three branches from a bush on them, and the scarlet roses we had brought.

We went in search of the Tilches, in whose name I remembered seeing a pavilion, with Bernard. After some rooting around, I reached the area where these individual "temples" were. The Tilches' was a well-built little Palladian construction. I untwisted the wire holding the door closed and stepped into a cloud of old and new dust. There was an entrance, a marble stairway. The floor on the lower level consisted of slabs, side by side. The keeper, who had one blind, almost shut eye, joined his hands palm to palm and rested one ear on them, indicating the floor with his chin to let me know that they were all graves beneath our feet. So much dust had accumulated that it was only by the iron handles on the side of each tombstone that I could begin to make out how many graves there were. Square skylights let in intense sunshine from the world of the living.

The keeper fetched a broom made of twigs and began to brush the dust away so the names might become visible. The little subterranean chamber filled with gold dust. I could see nothing around me but began to make out letters on the ground. We choked on the dust and coughed. There was one loose square marble plaque: it read "Georges Tilche," my grandmother's brother, who died in '58. I gave up, seeing no point in breathing in more dust to read names of relatives I either didn't know or whose disappearance it was too late to mourn.

I did not find my mother's brother Gino, who died at nineteen. It now seemed a ritual to leave at least one stone unturned for my next trip to Alexandria.

I asked Tasula to guide me to the Sephardic synagogue on Nebi Daniel. "Mr. Joe" received us there. He was president of the Communauté Israélite, Grand Rabbinat, of Alexandria. Outside his office, on a slab of marble—more marble to commemorate the names of the dead—listing the founders, I found the name of my great-grandfather Oreste Pinto. A slight woman with wavy grey hair brushed close to the skull whom Tasula had introduced me to as a friend of Madame Cristina's asked me in French, "You are . . . *like here?*" I laughed, the euphemism struck me as droll. She said, "Oh, but one has to be careful, these days."

In the synagogue containing the twenty or so sephers from all the other synagogues of Alexandria that had been closed down, Mr. Joe, long-nosed, small-eyed, his scalp etched with skin cancers and age spots, in an impeccable chalk-striped navy blue wool three-piece suit, ambled about looking for a seat with my grandfather's name on it and there wasn't one: I was not a bit surprised, knowing he had probably never set foot in the synagogue.

I winked at Tasula. Mr. Joe asked whether I wanted to light a candle. It was the second time he suggested I do so. I had pretended not to hear him the first time, not knowing whether some ritual I knew nothing about might be involved: I did not want to offend him.

I spent an hour at Saint Saba, the Greek Orthodox Church across the street from where Cavafy had lived. He could see it from his windows. Leaving the bright sunshine, I entered what appeared to be a cave cushioned in shadow, lined with icons in ornate silver frames, and I sat on a bench enveloped in the peculiar light of fervor the place emanates, transported to his Alexandria, gradually discerning the geometry of the room as my eyes adjusted to the flicker of tall thin candles.

Back at the Elite, a Greek friend of Madame Cristina's who had dropped in, as she often did in the course of her morning rounds, sat next to me as I sipped coffee as though it were medicine that could restore all the energy lost negotiating the streets of Alexandria, the traffic, the merchants, the crossings. She began to tell me all about her unfortunate son's marriage, of his scheming avid wife. One interesting piece of information she conveyed to me, on hearing my name, was that she had known my grandfather Silvio's brother Carlo, the obstetrician who brought me into the world, and had sold him a collection of perfume bottles. I was so tired that I simply sat quietly as she babbled on. Finally, she must have realized I hadn't said a word; like a fire that goes out when it's not rekindled, she stopped, and got up to take her leave.

I waited for Madame Cristina to dismount from her raised throne behind the cash register. She came to sit at my right. We were joined by a Greek friend of hers, a dentist in the daytime, and at night, a singer who performs at Arab weddings and parties the songs of Frank Sinatra, Yves Montand, Tom Jones. He had doglike eyes, big jowls, a fundamental docility. When Madame Cristina got up to take a phone call, he confided to

me, "She is like a mother to me, may God spare her health."
Our lunch, ordered by Madame Cristina, arrived: onion soup,
veal scaloppine with wine and mashed potatoes (the last things
one would think of eating in Alexandria and for that very reason
the most exotic). I struggled to eat, but the Greek "son" ate
carefully and methodically all of the soup, which instead of
croutons had pieces of toasted Arabic bread in it; then all of the
scaloppine, and the mashed potatoes, pushing dollops of gravy
onto every forkful until his plate was clean. Madame Cristina
said she couldn't have what we were having because it was "too
heavy." I wondered what made her think that we would find it
light—perhaps she attributed greater digestive powers to our
youth. She wanted us to have the most expensive things on the
menu.

She herself ordered a piece of the famous fish Tasula and I
had bought at the market that morning. It came covered in a
buttery sauce. I noticed that although she was suffering from
the flu, she finished her portion.

When the dentist had finished eating, he kissed her on both
cheeks and left. "Poor thing," she said, "his friend ate by himself on the veranda, but they left together." I was astounded,
having noticed none of it. Madame Cristina approved of her
friend's secretive behavior. "For him," she explained, "not for
me: it wouldn't be good for him to be seen with his friend."

She produced a Polaroid of her only son, an antiques dealer
in Paris: a willowy man seated at a crystal table, partly obscured
from view by a vase filled with tuberoses. She spoke of Cavafy.
When he was still alive, she had seen him walking along the
street: his face was powdered, he wore a red silk scarf around
his neck, a black suit; he was, she said, "very ugly," and his
lover looked just like him . . . some thought he was Cavafy's

son. When he had visitors, he would tell his manservant to fetch either the pink glasses or the clear glasses. If he asked for the rose-colored glasses, the servant would know that he did not like his guests and so to bring out only a dish of olives; these he would then put into his mouth one after the other, so he wouldn't have to make conversation. If he asked for the clear glasses, many little dishes of *mezé* would arrive.

Madame Cristina maintains that he was very full of himself, even obnoxious, and liked to astound a gathering with his knowledge, and having done so, took instant leave so as not to mar the impression of his superiority. Cavafy's family was very affluent. His mother had wanted a girl, after having several boys, so she always dressed him as a girl. "That's why he became homosexual," Madame Cristina concluded, "and every time he made love to a man, he wrote on a piece of paper that he would never do so again, only to break his resolve soon after."

I left the Elite to go back to the Cecil, where I would be picked up by car and taken to meet Professor Nahwat Abdallah at Senghor University—the African Francophone university. Yusri the driver arrived on time and drove me a ridiculously short distance down the corniche. Having reached the smoked glass tower, the highest building in Alexandria, we turned onto an ascending ramp, up and up in a vertiginous spiral to the fifth floor. I had not been feeling well since just before lunch: the expedition with Tasula, the haggling over fish, the hopping over puddles and chickens, dodging cars, the strangely stilted conversation with the Greek dentist-crooner, the scaloppine, my evenings alone at the Cecil, my feeling of incompetence at not being able to salvage the atmosphere or the talk, had brought on a mighty headache, starting up either side of the base of the neck, and over the skull in a vibrating grip that somehow seemed to settle back into my throat.

Steeling myself to walk straight, I was ushered into Nahwat's enormous office—smoked glass windows, views of Fort Qait Bey, the horseshoe harbor, and the sea. I sat in a chair not knowing how I could make it through the meeting without avowing my indisposition. I tried to make conversation. The Senegalese president of the university, Nahwat's superior, came in clearly in the mood for a chat. He talked of the furniture some Alexandrian craftsmen were making for him—cheaper than in Senegal, he said, and better workmanship. They had offered to show him a sample, and before he knew it they had hauled a huge console up to his office. He was very pleased with this story and Nahwat was pleased that he was pleased—solicitous, motherly, protective, a woman deferring.

I was pleased not to have to speak, tried to smile. My headache grew. I felt nauseous. Soon the jovial president left, and I was left face to face with Nahwat. I smiled. I told her I was in Alex to research a travel article on the city, and to work on a book about my family. She said she was off on a little holiday with her family to Marsā Matrūh. Finally I could stand it no longer: I confessed that I felt so sick that I would have to return to the hotel immediately. She was surprised, but kind. A few months earlier it was she who had been in bed with the flu and unable to see me. I mustered all my strength to walk out of her office, cross the corridor, make it into the elevator, then into the car. We drove back down the dizzying ramp, and to the hotel.

I made it upstairs, put on my Chinese down jacket, slipped

into bed, and slept soundly for two hours. When I woke up, I realized that I would have to endure another solitary night at the Cecil. I called my friend Nini in Cairo, to find out whether she was still planning to come to Alex for a day. I told her of my sudden illness just when I was finally meeting her friend, whom she had so recommended to me, that afternoon. One needs a friend in every foreign city, I said. I had regretted my choice of staying at the Cecil, which was in the center of Alexandria, but too far from Rushdy and the house of my friend Gamila and her family, who had been so welcoming on my last trip. I had gone there nearly every night, after finishing my rounds of the city, revisiting family sites. Like a character in a film bent on making contrary statements, Nini said peremptorily that one did not need a friend in every foreign city.

She told me she planned to spend the thirty-first of December with her mother, whose health had been failing in the last year. Nini herself had a persistent cough which the doctors thought might be a chronic condition brought on by the pollution in Cairo. As we spoke, her daughter was watching the news and I heard the television din in the background. Two thousand soldiers had besieged Assiut, she reported in a high-pitched voice. Assiut, the fundamentalist stronghold. "It's civil war!" she shouted. Nini told me, "Leave, leave now. Leave Alexandria tomorrow afternoon: see the Roman theater in the morning, then go. What are you waiting for? Come to Cairo, at least you'll be closer to getting away." She communicated her alarm to me: she was not easily stirred, but I underestimated the effect her daughter could have on her. The next day they apologized for their exaggerated response, saying that the news as it had been reported had seemed to announce a serious crisis.

I put down the receiver and my thoughts skipped about

among the things I needed to do if I was to leave on the following day. I found I was relieved at the thought of leaving, didn't know why I had needed a pretext. What was the point of another three nights in Alexandria: a bad journey rarely rights itself. It was ruined by New Year's Eve that lay sullenly on the horizon as I tried not to think about it. I knew I didn't want to spend it by myself. Nini had said, "You still care about that?"

I packed my bags, changed my reservation at the Atlas in Cairo to the following night, asked the concierge to purchase a ticket for me on the two o'clock *turbini* express to Cairo. I woke up early, went to see the Roman theater, the catacombs at Kom el Shogafa, Pompey's Pillar. Then I asked the cabdriver to take me to a pastry shop I knew in the district of Ibrahimiya. A waiter there enumerated all the different types of pastries, which all looked similar; perhaps the difference lay in the type of nuts with which they were stuffed. I thought I would bring an assorted tray of them to my mother. I paid sixteen pounds at the counter, including two pastries for the driver and myself. He proffered a yellow tissue to me from his box of multicolored ones.

Time had stopped in the morning, and now suddenly it had vanished and I had to check out of the Cecil and get to the train station.

On the *turbini*, a little lunch tray was brought to me: an earthenware pot containing mutton stew, light green zucchini, tomatoes, a plate of Arabic rice very similar to the kind I had eaten throughout the years of my childhood—sauteed in oil, then steamed; a square tile of baklava steeped in honey. Hot tea. Fifteen Egyptian pounds.

The driver of the cab I got into at the station in Cairo said his was a "special" cab so I would have to pay more for the ride. I said I wouldn't, and realized I was getting used to bargaining. My voice and manner in negotiation had become firm. He said okay, and my eyes rested on the cobalt blue carpet lining his dashboard.

The Atlas Zamalek—home almost. Sleep. Wake-up call at five-thirty. Tea. Another tip to another waiter. Glass of water. Squeeze yukata into black bag. Piece of fabric gets stuck in zipper. Check out, pay. Cab waiting. As we roll slowly through the deserted streets cleaned for Rabin's summit with Arafat, he says, "Ticket all right? Money all right?" And after a pause, "Not all right, I drive you back same price."

Strada in Chianti. New Year's watching distant fireworks from a darkened room. The relief of swooning into bed early, falling asleep instantly . . . *Be not sad, be like the sun at midday.*

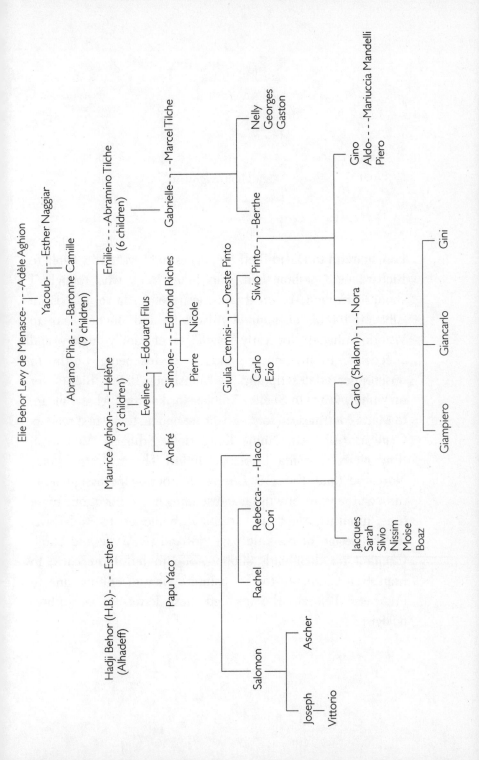

Acknowledgments

I am grateful to David Rieff for suggesting I write this book; to Richard de Combray and Joan Juliet Buck who thought I should write long before I had the nerve to do so; to Nissim Alhadeff for his account of Auschwitz and Buchenwald; to Vittorio Alhadeff for early fragments of family history and anecdotes; to my mother and father for being worthy of unsentimental description; to Monsignor Pierre Riches for his unholy faith; to Shelley Wanger for knowing what I mean; to Maria Matthiessen for her delicate pencil; to my first readers Giancarlo Alhadeff, Janine King, Holly Brubach, Aldo Busi, Amy Hertz, Barbara Jakobson, Judith Thurman; to Nancy Novogrod (and *Travel & Leisure*) for bestowing assignments through the years of writing and sending me to Egypt one more time; to all who lent me books and memories; to Paul Davis for the design of the title page; to Andrew Wylie and Sarah Chalfant for their early support, and to Jeff Posternack; to Francesco Clemente for his painter's view of editing; and to Francesco Pellizzi, who inspired these letters to an anthropologist.

About the Author

Gini Alhadeff was born in Alexandria, Egypt. She founded the literary magazines *Normal* and *XXIst Century*. She lives in New York City and in Strada in Chianti.